Decorative Painting
for the first time®

Decorative Painting
for the first time®

Sterling Publishing Co., Inc. New York
A Sterling/Chapelle Book

Chapelle, Ltd.:

Jo Packham
Sara Toliver
Cindy Stoeckl

Editor: Laura Best
Art Director: Karla Haberstich
Copy Editor: Marilyn Goff
Staff: Kelly Ashkettle, Areta Bingham,
Donna Chambers, Emily Frandsen,
Lana Hall, Mackenzie Johnson,
Susan Jorgensen, Jennifer Luman,
Melissa Maynard, Barbara Milburn,
Lecia Monsen, Suzy Skadburg,
Kim Taylor, Desirée Wybrow

If you have any questions or comments, contact:
Chapelle, Ltd., Inc.,
P.O. Box 9252, Ogden, UT 84409
(801) 621-2777 • (801) 621-2788 Fax
e-mail: chapelle@chapelleltd.com
web site: chapelleltd.com

Library of Congress Cataloging-in-Publication Data
Decorative painting for the first time / Plaid.
    p. cm.
"A Sterling/Chapelle Book."
Includes index.
ISBN 1-4027-0261-2
 1. Painting—Technique. 2. Decoration and ornament. I. Plaid
Enterprises.
TT385 .D412 2003
745.7'23—dc22
                                          2003017488

10 9 8 7 6 5 4 3 2 1

Published in paperback in 2005 by Sterling Publishing Co., Inc.
387 Park Avenue South, New York, NY 10016
© 2004 by Plaid
Distributed in Canada by Sterling Publishing
℅ Canadian Manda Group, 165 Dufferin Street
Toronto, Ontario, Canada M6K 3H6
Distributed in Great Britain by Chrysalis Books Group PLC,
The Chrysalis Building, Bramley Road, London W10 6SP, England
Distributed in Australia by Capricorn Link (Australia) Pty. Ltd.
P.O. Box 704, Windsor, NSW 2756, Australia
Printed and Bound in China
All Rights Reserved

Sterling ISBN 1-4027-0261-2   Hardcover
        ISBN 1-4027-2764-X   Paperback

For information about custom editions, special sales, premium and
corporate purchases, please contact Sterling Special Sales
Department at 800-805-5489 or specialsales@sterlingpub.com.

Plaid, Inc.

Editor: Mickey Baskett

If you have any questions or comments, contact:
Plaid Enterprises, Inc. • Norcross, GA 30091-7600
(800) 842-4197 • web site: plaidonline.com

Special thank-you to the Artists.

Plaid Enterprises, Inc., prides itself in having a team of the best artists in the country. These artists teach across the country, appear on television, demonstrate at trade shows, contribute to magazines, and help promote the FolkArt line of paint. Plaid is most grateful to the wonderful group of artists who shared their painting knowledge and contributed their projects to make this book possible.

Thank you:
Gigi Smith-Burns, Donna Dewberry, Karen Embry, Priscilla Hauser, Susan Kelley, Kathi Malarchuk, Barbara Mansfield, Mary McCullah, Pat McIntosh, Donna Lee Parella, Terri Ridenour, Laraine Short, Chris Stokes, Tasha Yates

Due to the limited space available, we must print our patterns at a reduced size in order to give our patrons the maximum number of patterns possible in our publications. We believe the quality and quantity of our patterns will compensate for any inconvenience this may cause.

How to use this book

Whether or not you have done decorative painting in the past, you will soon become an expert by following the instructions provided in this book. The projects herein have been carefully ordered, starting with the most basic techniques and finishing with more-advanced maneuvers. As you complete one project and move on to the next, you will find that each technique builds upon that which was taught in a previous project. Should you choose to make a project out of sequence, you may find that you need to review the instructions for the project you skipped.

Section 1: Painting basics familiarizes you with the basic tools and supplies needed to begin decorative painting.

Section 2: Basic techniques introduces the building blocks necessary for painting projects. Each project introduces a new technique. If you jump ahead to a project out of sequence, you may find you have skipped a project which introduced a technique you now need to use. Though the provided information allows you to make the projects as they are pictured, feel free to alter any elements of the design as you desire.

Section 3: Beyond the basics expands on the techniques learned in Section 2 with projects that are a bit more complex. Do not be intimidated by what you see. You will have learned all the basic techniques that are required to make these projects.

Section 4: The gallery displays advanced ideas and designs by professionals in the field of painting to inspire you to continue in the craft.

The purpose of this book is to provide a starting point and to teach basic skills. The more you practice, the more comfortable you will feel. Allow yourself a reasonable amount of time to complete your first project—remember this is your first time. After you have completed the first few projects, you will be surprised by how quickly you will be able to decorative paint. Take pride in the talents you are developing and the unique and memorable projects that only you can create.

Table of Contents

Section 3:

Beyond the basics—76

Section 4:

The gallery—102

Section 1: Painting basics

General instructions—supplies

Paints

Paints are the most important supply when painting. Consider the surface you are painting when choosing your paint.

Acrylic craft paints—are richly pigmented paints that have been formulated for design painting purposes. They are ready to use with no mixing required. While there are many subtle premixed shades, there are also pure, intense, universal pigment colors that are true to the nature of standard pigments. These paints can be used on almost any type of surface.

Acrylic enamels for glass—are waterbased, nontoxic, and dry to an opaque finish and gloss sheen. Glass and ceramic pieces painted with these enamels can be hand-washed and are top-rack dishwasher safe. Do not paint within ⅛" of top rim of glasses or mugs or use in direct contact with food. Reverse-painting on the backs of clear glass plates is recommended if plates are to be used with food.

Enamel clear medium—can be used to create floating effects without losing adhesion on the glass. It can be used on glass and glazed ceramics in a similar fashion to floating medium. You can also mix 1:1 with paint to create a transparent paint.

Indoor/outdoor acrylic enamels—are durable, high-gloss enamels. These paints are weather resistant, making them usable for projects such as mailboxes, garden signs, and house numbers.

Paints for plastic—are formulated to stay on hard, rigid plastic (styrene, acrylic, ABS) and not chip off like conventional acrylics. Once dry, these acrylic paints are permanent. They are easy to use and dry quickly. They are water-resistant so they can be used for outdoor as well as indoor projects.

Mediums

Blending gel medium—makes blending of paint colors easier. It keeps paints moist, giving more time to shade and highlight before drying.

Crackle medium—creates what normally takes wind and weather many years. This water-based, nontoxic medium is easy to use on furniture and decorative accessories. When applied over a dry acrylic base coat, it forms cracks instantly.

Extender—when mixed with paint, extends drying time and adds transparency for floating, blending, and washing colors. Creates effects from transparent to opaque without reducing color intensity.

Floating medium—is used instead of water for floating, shading, or highlighting. It is easier to float a color with medium than water because it allows more control, and the medium will not run like water.

Frosting medium—creates frosted effects on clear or colored glass, plastic, or candles.

Glass & tile medium—is used when painting on glass, tile, or other slick surfaces. It gives a translucent surface with "more tooth" on which to paint, reducing the tendency of paint to slide around. It increases the durability of paint on these surfaces and provides a matte finish on both nonporous and porous materials. Though the surface can be hand-washed, use it on items that are for decorative purposes only.

Glazing medium—when mixed with acrylic paint, gives the perfect consistency to a topcoat that can be textured with other techniques. It can also be used as an antiquing medium.

Painting medium—is added to acrylic paints to change their properties so they can be used for specific functions such as painting on glass and fabrics or antiquing.

Textile medium—creates permanent, washable, painted effects on fabric. When mixed with acrylic paint, the medium allows the paint to penetrate fibers while retaining softness.

Thickener—is mixed with paint to create transparent colors while maintaining a thick flow and consistency. It is also used for painted faux finishes.

Brushes

Decorative painting uses "artist brushes." These are made of natural hairs or high-quality synthetic hairs. Brush quality is important to successfully achieve a painted design, so shop for the best you can afford. The size of the brush to use depends on the size of the area to be painted.

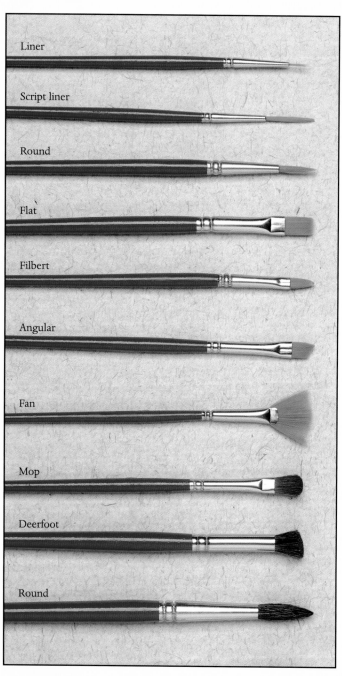

Flat, round, and liner brushes are the most important brushes to purchases. You could do all your decorative painting with these three brushes alone. However, as with most hobbies and crafts, as you become more proficient, you find yourself requiring more refined tools.

Angulars—are flat brushes with the bristles cut at an angle. They are used to paint fine chiseled edges, curved strokes, and to blend.

Deerfoot brushes—are round brushes with bristles cut at an angle. They are used for shading, stippling, and adding texture.

Fans—are finishing brushes that are rarely loaded with paint. They are traditionally used clean and dry.

Filberts—are flat brushes with a rounded tip. Because the tips are rounded, they can make fine chiseled lines. They are also helpful for curved stripes, filling in, and blending.

Flats—are rectangular in shape with long bristles. The chiseled edge makes fine lines while the flat edge makes wide strokes. They can carry a large quantity of paint without having to reload often. Flats can be used for base-coating, double-loading, floating, and washing.

Liners—are round and thin brushes used to paint small areas. Scrollers and script liners have longer bristles. They are used to paint fine lines and calligraphic strokes. Detail work such as outlining, facial features, tendrils, veins in leaves and flowers, and other fine work is done with these brushes.

Mops—are round brushes with soft long bristles. They are used for smoothing, softening, and blending edges.

Rounds—have a round ferrule and the bristles taper to a fine point at the tip. These brushes are used not only in base-coating, but are helpful with strokework. The fine tip works well for painting details and tiny spaces.

Scruffy brushes—are wide rectangular brushes with short bristles. They can be purchased or you can simply use a damaged or worn-out flat brush. They cannot be used for strokes, but work well for pouncing, stippling, dry-brushing, or dabbing.

Sponge brushes—are used for evenly applying base coats on project surfaces before decorative painting is applied. Sponge brushes, sometimes referred to as foam brushes, are also used for applying finishing coats.

Stencil brushes—are round brushes with either soft or stiff bristles. These brushes need very little paint loaded onto them. Excess paint is dabbed off onto a paper towel before applying it to project surface. Paint is applied to project either with a pouncing motion or a circular motion.

Stencil rollers—are made of foam and are specifically designed with tapered ends to prevent paint ridges. They are ideal for achieving a quick background.

Wash brushes—are large flat brushes used to apply basecoat, washes, and finishes.

Scroller

Scruffy

Wash

Flat

Stencil

Brush care & cleanup

Brushes must be properly cleaned and cared for. A new, quality brush has sizing in it to hold the bristles in place. Before painting, remove the sizing by gently rolling bristles between your fingers. Then thoroughly clean brush with water.

After the painting is complete, wash the brush, being careful not to abuse bristles. Work bristles back and forth in a brush cleaner. A liquid brush cleaner cleans wet or dried paint from bristles and keeps brushes groomed between uses. Once paint is removed, leave the cleaner in the bristles and shape them with your fingers. Rinse the brush again before painting.

Soft cloth—is used for wiping brushes since rough paper towels can damage bristles.

Water basin—is used with clean water for rinsing brushes and provides a surface on which to rest brushes, keeping the ferrules and handles out of water. A container with a ridged bottom helps clean bristles.

General instructions—prepare

Painting surfaces

Before beginning a project, read through the instructions. Follow the steps in order. Prepare the project surface with primer or base-paint before applying patterns and paint. Projects painted without primer can peel, crack, or powder off. Do not touch areas to be painted as skin oil can harm paint's adhesion.

When sanding between coats of primer, paint, or varnish, check surface for smoothness. If surface appears to be scratched after sanding, you are either, using sandpaper that is too coarse, or sanding before product is dry. If this happens, let the surface dry, and sand again. Use tack cloth to wipe away dust after each sanding.

Fabric

Prewash and dry fabric to remove any sizing that comes in new fabric and to guard against shrinkage from later washings. This will also help paint bond better with fibers. Do not use a fabric softener. Before painting, cover cardboard with plastic wrap and insert directly behind the area to be painted to protect other layers of fabric from paint and to provide a firm surface on which to paint When painting on fabric, mix paints with textile medium on the palette.

Glass & ceramic

Use rubbing alcohol to clean a glass surface. Apply a glass and tile medium to these nonporous surfaces to give the project some "tooth" for the paint to hold onto.

Metal

An enamel is the best type of paint to use on metal to ensure that the design will not peel off. Tin has long been used for painting (previously called "tole" painting), and features items such as watering cans, buckets, kitchen scoops, and garden tools. Today, even rusted tin is popular. Wrought iron has also become more popular with greater interest in yard and garden decor.

New tin

Some new tins may need no preparation. However, galvanized tin has an oily film that must be removed before painting. Using a sponge or soft cloth, clean the item with a solution of water and vinegar. Do not immerse the piece in water as water can be trapped in tight areas of the piece, causing problems later. Rinse well and dry thoroughly. Painted or enameled tin requires damp sponging with water, then drying.

Old metal

Sand surface or rub with steel wool to remove loose paint or rust and smooth imperfections. Wipe well with a cloth dampened in turpentine. Let dry. Apply a metal primer. Let primer dry thoroughly, then sand lightly with fine-grade sandpaper. Wipe with a tack cloth.

Plastic

Use rubbing alcohol to clean the surface and remove static charge. Since clear plastic is transparent, you can tape pattern inside rather than transferring it. Since most acrylic paints will not stick to plastic when dry, use a paint formulated for use on plastic or first mist plastic pieces with a matte acrylic sealer.

Slate

Unpolished stone is slightly porous so paint easily adheres to it. Blackboard slate is denser and therefore less porous. Prepare slate by lightly misting the surface with a matte sealer.

Terra-cotta

Wash and dry, if necessary, with mild soap and water. If dirt is stubborn, use a water/vinegar solution. If you plan to plant directly into a painted pot, coat the inside of the pot with an outdoor sealer so water and moisture will not soak through.

Wood

Be certain the surface is clean and free from dirt and oil. Sand new wood with 120-grit sandpaper until surface appears smooth, then use 220-grit sandpaper to finish. Sand with the grain of the wood.

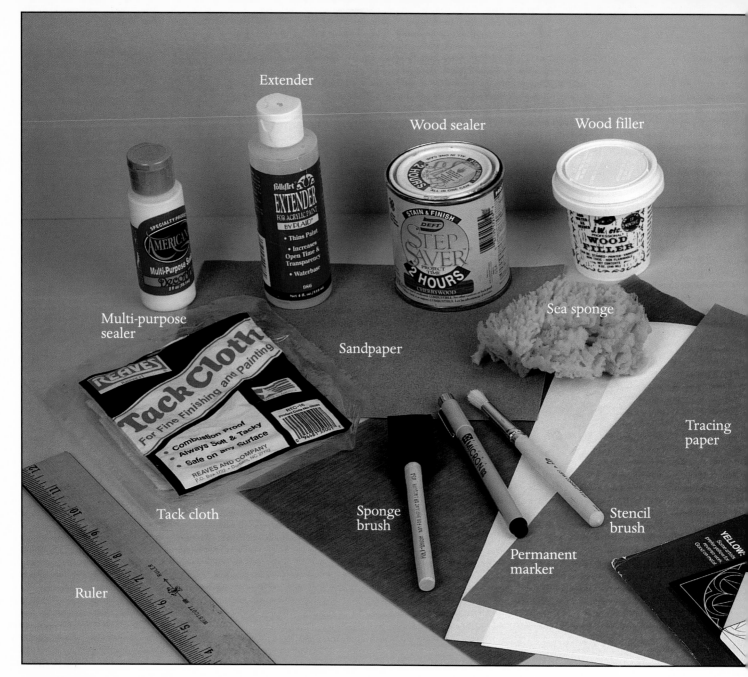

Extender

Wood sealer

Wood filler

Multi-purpose
sealer

Sea sponge

Sandpaper

Tracing
paper

Tack cloth

Sponge
brush

Stencil
brush

Permanent
marker

Ruler

Miscellaneous supplies

Art eraser—to remove pattern lines

Blow dryer—to speed drying

Extender—to slow drying time

Low-tack masking tape—to secure patterns

Multi-purpose sealer—to prepare surface
before painting

Palette knife—to mix paints

Paper towels—to clean up

Pencil—to aid in transferring patterns

Permanent marker—to trace patterns

Ruler—to measure placement

Sanding ovals—to remove rough spots from
painting surfaces

Sandpaper—to remove rough spots from
painting surfaces

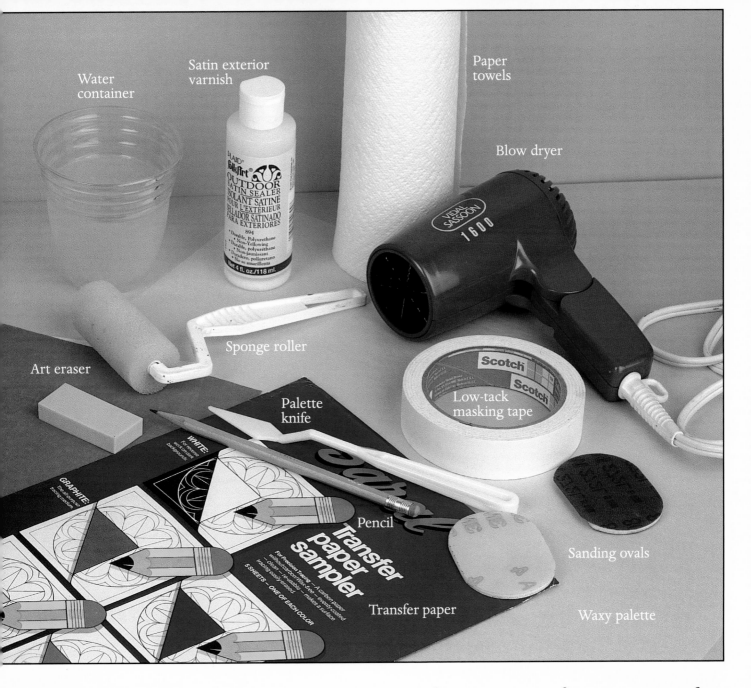

Water container

Satin exterior varnish

Paper towels

Blow dryer

Sponge roller

Art eraser

Palette knife

Scotch
Scotch
Low-tack masking tape

Pencil

Transfer paper sampler

Sanding ovals

Transfer paper

Waxy palette

Satin exterior varnish—to protect projects

Sea sponge—to sponge-paint

Sponge brush—to apply paint or varnish

Sponge roller—to apply paint or varnish

Stencil brush—to spatter

Tack cloth—to remove dust after sanding

Tracing paper—to trace patterns from book

Transfer paper—to transfer patterns onto surface

Water container—to rinse brushes

Waxy palette—to arrange and mix paints

Wood filler—to fill holes and gaps in wood

Wood sealer—to prepare surface before painting

(See individual project instructions for additional supplies needed.)

Transfer tools

Pencil—is used to trace patterns from the book or to transfer a pattern onto a prepared surface. A soft-leaded #2 pencil works best for tracing.

Photocopier & paper—are used to enlarge and copy patterns from the book to then transfer onto painting surface.

Stylus—is a pencil-like tool used to transfer a traced or photocopied design onto a prepared surface. A pencil or a ballpoint pen with no ink may also be used.

Tracing paper—is used to trace patterns from the book to keep the book intact. Choose a tracing paper that is as transparent as possible for carefully tracing designs.

Transfer paper—is used to transfer a traced or photocopied pattern onto the project surface. It comes with either a light or a dark velvet coating. Choose transfer paper that has a water-soluble coating in a color that will be visible on the base-coat color of the project surface.

Transfer patterns

Project patterns are included in this book. To keep these pages intact, photocopy them, enlarging or reducing as necessary to fit surface.

To trace, place tracing paper over pattern. Secure with low-tack masking tape. Using a pencil, trace the major design elements onto tracing paper. Use the detailed pattern and the photograph as guides when you paint.

To transfer, position traced or photocopied pattern on project, securing one side with masking tape. Slip transfer paper between pattern and project surface. Make certain that the velvet coating is against the base-painted surface. Using a stylus, retrace pattern lines with enough pressure to transfer the lines but not so much as to indent the surface. Use dark transfer paper for light surfaces and light (white) transfer paper for dark surfaces.

Another transfer option would be to use chalk. Rub chalk across the back of the pattern, place on prepared surface, and retrace the pattern lines with a stylus.

When using a pattern, first transfer only the main outline of the design onto the project to be base-painted. After the base-painting is dry, transfer the pattern details onto the design for painting, shading, and highlighting.

General instructions—
paint design

Palette

Palettes differ, from disposable plates and palette papers to wood or plastic reusable artists' palettes. Regardless of the material, palettes are used for laying out paints, loading brushes, and blending paints into the brushes.

Paints are squeezed onto a palette into a nickel-sized puddle for easy access when loading a brush. The palette is also used to mix paints with water, other colors, or painting mediums.

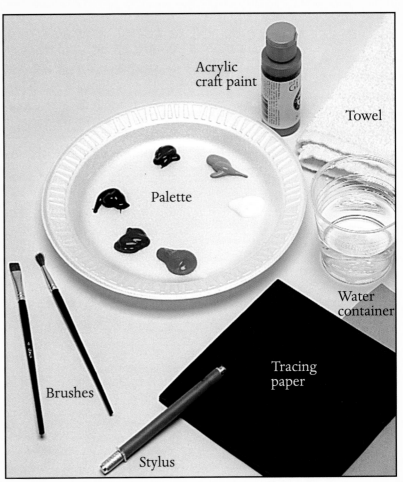

Acrylic craft paint

Towel

Palette

Water container

Brushes

Tracing paper

Stylus

Palette knife

A palette knife is used for both mixing and applying paint. Palette knives come in two different styles. Both have long flat blades, but one style has an elevated handle to help keep hand out of paint.

A good palette knife should be thin and flexible when it touches the project surface. Palette knives can have metal or plastic blades, depending on the cost and durability needed.

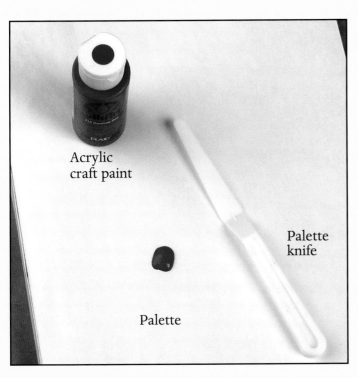

Acrylic craft paint

Palette knife

Palette

Loading a flat or filbert brush

1. Squeeze a small puddle of paint onto palette. Place brush at edge of puddle. Pull paint out from edge of puddle with brush, loading one side of brush.

2. Flip brush over and repeat to load other side. Continue flipping brush and brushing back and forth on palette to fully load bristles.

Loading a liner or scroller

1. Squeeze a small puddle of paint onto palette and dilute it at one edge with water. Paint must be "thinned" to an "inky" consistency so that it flows.

2. Pull liner along diluted edge of puddle, loading paint into bristles. Twirl bristles at edge of puddle to sharpen point.

Loading a round brush

1. Squeeze a small puddle of paint onto palette. Hold brush at edge of puddle. Push brush straight down into puddle.

Loading a scruffy brush

1. Squeeze a small puddle of paint onto palette. Hold brush at edge of puddle. Push brush straight down. Rotate brush. Be certain bristles are loaded.

Using a painting worksheet

Paint worksheets demonstrate a variety of painting techniques and allow you to practice a stroke before attempting it on your project surface. Some worksheets are available with a protective plastic coating so you can paint directly on it, then wipe it clean when finished. The worksheets in this book can be used similarly. Color-copy the worksheet, then cover it with clear plastic wrap, or a sheet of acetate.

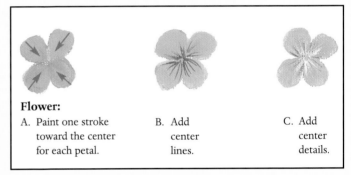

Flower:
A. Paint one stroke toward the center for each petal.
B. Add center lines.
C. Add center details.

1. Though worksheets group design elements together, follow the succession in alphabetical order. Arrows may be added to the examples to show the way the stroke should be done.

2. Apply strokes, following directions of arrows. Paint petals first, then center, then details.

Basic Brush Strokes Worksheet

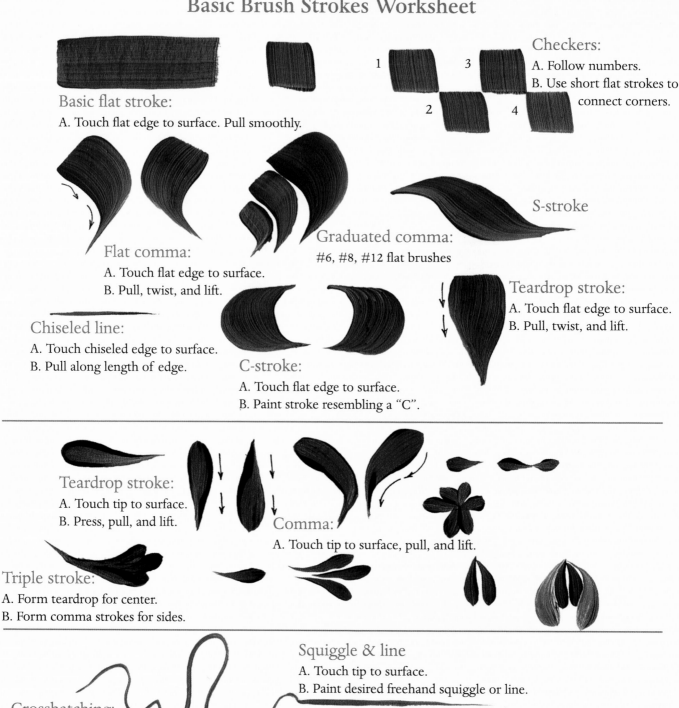

Flats

Basic flat stroke:
A. Touch flat edge to surface. Pull smoothly.

Checkers:
A. Follow numbers.
B. Use short flat strokes to connect corners.

1 3
2 4

Flat comma:
A. Touch flat edge to surface.
B. Pull, twist, and lift.

Graduated comma:
#6, #8, #12 flat brushes

S-stroke

Teardrop stroke:
A. Touch flat edge to surface.
B. Pull, twist, and lift.

Chiseled line:
A. Touch chiseled edge to surface.
B. Pull along length of edge.

C-stroke:
A. Touch flat edge to surface.
B. Paint stroke resembling a "C".

Rounds

Teardrop stroke:
A. Touch tip to surface.
B. Press, pull, and lift.

Comma:
A. Touch tip to surface, pull, and lift.

Triple stroke:
A. Form teardrop for center.
B. Form comma strokes for sides.

Liners

Squiggle & line
A. Touch tip to surface.
B. Paint desired freehand squiggle or line.

Crosshatching:
A. Touch liner tip to surface.
B. Crisscross with thin lines.

Lettering:
A. Touch tip to surface.
B. Always pull brush toward you.

Heart:
A. Connect dots and pull down from center.

Dots:
A. Load handle end of brush.
B. Make dots with one load.

22

General instructions—finish

Erase remaining pattern lines. Use a high-quality varnish or sealer. Choose sealers that are nonyellowing and quick-drying. Using a tack cloth, remove lint, dust, or dirt before applying.

If project is new wood and was stained or glazed, the wood will soak up most of the first coat of finish, requiring more coats than a painted surface. If project is to be used outdoors or receive heavy traffic, apply a protective sealer such as polyurethane. Waterproof exterior acrylics need not be varnished.

Acrylic sealer—protects projects after final paint is dry. Apply 2–3 coats.

Aerosol finish—is sprayed onto surfaces to seal and protect against moisture, soil, and dust. Spray dry project with sealer. Spray several times to provide smooth finish. Let dry between coats. Sand surface with wet 400-grit sandpaper or with a fine-grade steel wool. Tack away dust.

Brush-on water-based varnish—protects, seals, and offers resistance from scratches and water spotting. Apply finish with a sponge brush after paint has dried.

To achieve a soft finish on large items, apply water-based varnish with a sponge roller. Do not worry about bubbles; with repeated rollings, the bubbles will vanish. Roll until varnish is near dry.

Outdoor varnish—should be used if the project will be placed out-of-doors. Apply 2–3 coats after paint has dried for 48 hours.

Finishing tips

- Sign and date your project after completion.

- If project is too shiny after finish coats are dry, buff with fine-grade steel wool or water-moistened 400-grit sandpaper.

Dry & cure

After applying paints to glass surfaces, allow paints to cure 21 days before using—OR—bake. To bake, let paint dry one hour, then place in a cool oven. Heat oven to 350° and bake projects for 30 minutes. Allow oven to cool with project in it.

Section 2: Basic techniques

1
technique

What you need to get started:

Painting surface:
Clear glass platter,
  size of your choosing

Acrylic enamel for glass:
Metallic Gold

Brush:
Liner: #3

Additional supplies:
Masking tape
Palette
Rubbing alcohol
Transfer tools

How do I paint a scroll?

Whether painting a line, curve, or scroll, the basic technique is the same for each stroke.

Here's how:

1. Select a liner or flat brush the width of the desired line. Load one side of brush with "inky" paint. Flip brush over and load other side. Continue flipping brush and brushing back and forth on palette to fully load bristles.

2. Hold brush perpendicular to surface. Place little finger on surface to guide hand. The wrist should not touch the surface. Apply steady pressure keeping line consistent.

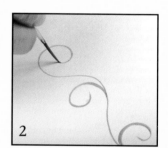

Filigree Platter

Designed by Pat McIntosh

Using the technique:

1. Refer to *General instructions—prepare* on pages 14–18. Prepare glass area to be painted. Let dry.

2. Enlarge Filigree Pattern on page 27 to fit platter. Repeat pattern to fit around rim. Tape pattern on front side of platter. Turn platter over to paint.

3. Refer to *General instructions—paint design* on pages 19–22. Using liner, paint design on back side of platter with Metallic Gold, following pattern lines.

4. Refer to *General instructions—finish* on page 23. Sign project. Let paint dry and cure before use.

Filigree Pattern

Enlarge as desired.

2–3 techniques

What you need to get started:

Painting surface:
Wooden frame,
   size of your choosing

Acrylic craft paints:
Blue Ink
Green Meadows
Napthol Crimson
Wicker White

Brushes:
Flat: #10
Round: #3
Sponge: 1"

Additional supplies:
Brush-on water-based
   varnish, satin
Palette
Pencil (optional)
Sandpaper
Tack cloth

technique 2: How do I base-paint?

The base coat is the first covering of paint. To base-paint means to cover an area with several initial coats of paint.

Here's how:

1. Use largest flat or sponge brush possible for surface to be painted.

2. Apply paint in long smooth strokes for even coverage. Let dry between each coat.

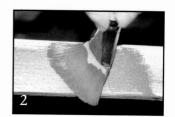

technique 3: How do I use a wash?

To enhance a painted design, apply a layer of transparent color (paint thinned with water) over the dry base coat.

Here's how:

1. Make a wash by mixing paint plus water 1:4 on the palette.

2. Load brush with wash and use long smooth strokes for an even coverage.

Picture Perfect

Designed by Pat McIntosh

Using the techniques:

1. Refer to *General instructions—prepare* on pages 14–18. Prepare wood area to be painted.

2. Using sponge, base-paint frame with Wicker White. Let dry.

3. Using pencil, lightly draw lines where stripes will be before painting. These will guide your strokes.

4. Refer to *General instructions—paint design* on pages 19–22. Make washes on palette with Blue Ink, Green Meadows, and Napthol Crimson.

5. Using flat, paint wide stripes with variety of washes. Let dry.

6. Using round, paint narrow stripes with variety of washes. Let dry.

7. Refer to *General instructions—finish* on page 23. Sign project.

8. Apply varnish, following the manufacturer's instructions.

Painting surfaces:
White ceramic bathroom
   pieces

Acrylic enamels for glass:
Italian Sage
Yellow Ochre

Brushes:
Flats: #6, #12

Additional supplies:
Palette
Rubbing alcohol
Transfer tools

What does the chiseled edge of a brush do?

When painting straight lines, the chiseled (pointed) bristle tips of a brush bring the greatest control. The more pressure applied, the wider the line produced.

Here's how:

1. Load flat fully with paint to avoid running out while pulling along the line. Keeping brush perpendicular to the surface, pull along length of chiseled edge.

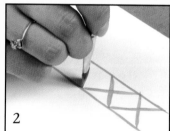

2. Load brush as needed and continue pulling smooth even strokes to keep the lines consistent.

Palm Trees Bathroom Set

Designed by Pat McIntosh

Using the technique:

1. Refer to *General instructions—prepare* on pages 14–18. Prepare ceramic area to be painted. Let dry.

2. Enlarge Palm Trees Patterns on page 31 to fit bathroom pieces. Transfer patterns onto pieces. Repeat patterns as desired to fit pieces.

3. Refer to *General instructions—paint design* on pages 19–22. Using #6 flat, paint bamboo border around bottom of desired pieces with Yellow Ochre.

4. Using chiseled edge, paint trunk with Italian Sage. While pulling brush in an upward motion, turn brush on its side to make trunk thinner. Paint palm fronds in the same manner, working from the center outward.

5. Using chiseled edge of fully-loaded #12 flat, paint ground with Italian Sage. Apply pressure to flatten brush where ground is to be wider.

6. Refer to *General instructions—finish* on page 23. Sign project.

7. Let paint dry and cure before use.

Palm Trees Patterns

Enlarge as desired.

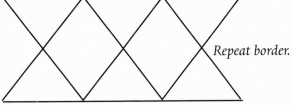

Repeat border.

Painting surface:
Glass goblet,
    size of your choosing

Acrylic enamels for glass:
Fresh Foliage
Hydrangea
Licorice
School Bus Yellow
Yellow Ochre

Brushes:
Filberts: #2, #6
Liner: #1

Additional supplies:
Masking tape
Palette
Transfer tools

How do I "pat" with a filbert brush?

The tips of a filbert brush are rounded, which makes fine chiseled lines. Rounded tips do not leave noticeable start and stop marks. When painting with a filbert a "raised" texture is formed.

Here's how:

1. Using a loaded filbert and working from the center of design out, pat brush up and down on project. Do not go back over area until paint is dry to avoid disturbing the raised texture created with patting.

Flower Goblet

Designed by Barbara Mansfield

Using the technique:

1. Refer to *General instructions—prepare* on pages 14–18. Prepare glass area to be painted.

2. Enlarge Daisy Patterns on page 33 to fit goblet. Tape pattern inside goblet, facing outward.

3. Refer to *General instructions—paint design* on pages 19–22. Refer to Daisy Painting Worksheet on page 33. Using #6 filbert, paint flower petals with Hydrangea.

4. Using #2 filbert, lighten centers with Yellow Ochre, then School Bus Yellow.

5. Using liner, pull in stems and leaves with Fresh Foliage.

6. Using handle end of brush, dot glass randomly with Licorice. Dip into paint after each touch.

7. Using #6 filbert, paint goblet foot with Hydrangea. Let dry.

8. Using #2 filbert, paint foot rim with Licorice. Let dry.

9. Refer to *General instructions—finish* on page 23. Sign project.

10. Let paint dry and cure before use.

Daisy Patterns

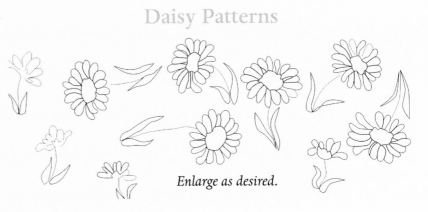

Enlarge as desired.

Daisy Painting Worksheet

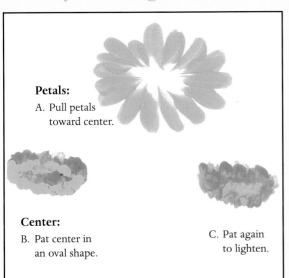

Petals:
A. Pull petals toward center.

Center:
B. Pat center in an oval shape.

C. Pat again to lighten.

What you need to get started:

Painting surface:
Wooden recipe box, 5" x 3"

Acrylic craft paints:
Medium Yellow
Mystic Green
Sky Blue
Thicket
Vivid Violet
Wicker White

Brushes:
Liner: #1
Rounds: #6, #8
Sponge: 1"

Additional supplies:
Brush-on water-based
    varnish, satin
Masking tape
Palette
Paper towel
Pencil
Ruler
Sandpaper
Stylus
Tack cloth
Transfer tools

technique 6:
How do I double-load a brush?

Double-loading is a simple way to fill a brush with two colors, creating a shaded look with just one stroke. When the two colors are brought onto the brush, a third color is formed in the brush center.

Here's how:

1. Touch one side of brush (i.e. side-load) into paint color. Touch opposite side into another color.

2. Paint will be definitely separated on brush.

3. Stroke brush to blend colors at brush center.

4. Colors should remain unblended on corners and form a middle value in the center.

technique 7:
How do I mask-off an area?

By applying tape across a dry base-painted surface, crisp lines can be painted between adjacent areas.

Here's how:

1. With ruler and pencil, mark lines for tape to run against. Apply tape smoothly along the lines. Be certain to securely press down tape edges to prevent paint from seeping underneath. Paint untaped areas (do not worry about paint overlapping tape). Remove tape before paint is dry.

Clematis Recipe Box

Designed by Barbara Mansfield

Using the techniques:

1. Refer to *General instructions—prepare* on pages 14–18. Prepare wood areas to be painted.

2. Using sponge, base-paint box and lid with Sky Blue. Let dry.

3. Mask-off around sides of box to expose narrow edging areas around top and bottom of area.

4. Using sponge, paint the edging with Thicket. Let dry.

5. Enlarge Clematis Patterns. Transfer patterns onto box. Repeat patterns to fit completely around box.

6. Refer to *General instructions—paint design* on pages 19–22. Refer to Clematis Painting Worksheet on page 37. Double-load #8 round with Vivid Violet and Wicker White. Place brush tip on surface and pull just a tiny bit to create pointed end of petal. Flatten bristles, then come back up on tip at flower center.

Top

Front

Enlarge 235%.

Sides

Back

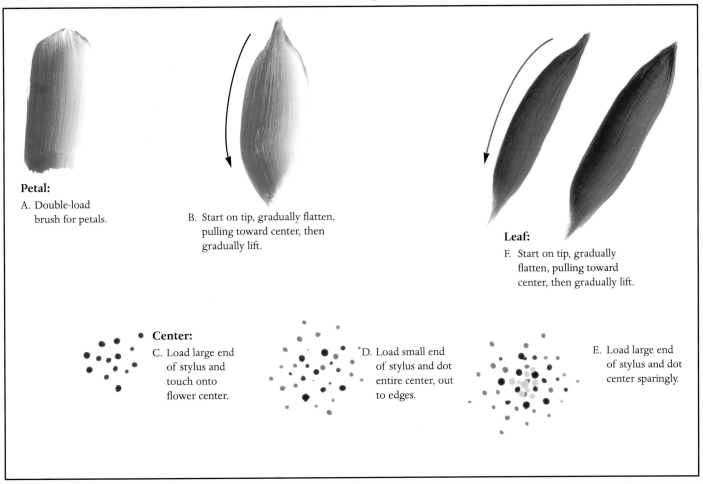

Petal:

A. Double-load brush for petals.

B. Start on tip, gradually flatten, pulling toward center, then gradually lift.

Leaf:

F. Start on tip, gradually flatten, pulling toward center, then gradually lift.

Center:

C. Load large end of stylus and touch onto flower center.

D. Load small end of stylus and dot entire center, out to edges.

E. Load large end of stylus and dot center sparingly.

7. Repeat petals all around the center. paint all flower petals.

8. Dip large end of stylus in Thicket and tap dots in flower centers.

9. Dip small end of stylus in Mystic Green and tap dots in flower center covering a larger area of center.

10. Dip large end of stylus in Medium Yellow and tap dots in flower center covering a small area.

11. Using liner, paint vine lines from flower to flower with Thicket.

12. Double-load #6 round with Mystic Green and Thicket. Stroke leaves.

13. Refer to *General instructions—finish* on page 23. Sign project.

14. Apply varnish, following manufacturer's instructions. Let dry.

8
technique

What you need to get started:

Painting surface:
Round wooden wall clock, 14½" dia.

Acrylic craft paints:
Burnt Carmine
Country Twill
Olive Green
Pure Gold (Metallic)
Taffy

Brushes:
Angular: ⅜"
Liners: #1, #4
Round: #3
Sponge: 2"

Additional supplies:
Brush-on water-based varnish, satin
Clockwork
Extender
Floating medium
Palette
Sandpaper
Tack cloth
Transfer tools
Water-based wood sealer

Floating is the technique of loading paint onto only one side of a brush. As paint is stroked onto the design, color drifts softly across bristles, flowing into nothing on the opposite side.

Here's how:

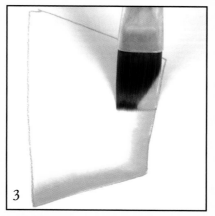

1. Fully-load complete brush with floating medium. Blot off excess. Side-load brush with color by pulling brush edge along puddle. Load only ⅓–½ of brush.

2. Brush back and forth on the palette to blend color into brush.

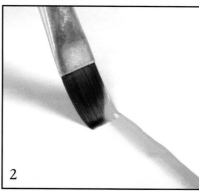

3. Pull brush along edges in design area. Color should be on the edge and fade as it reaches the center.

Enlarge 560%.

Pieces of Time Clock

Designed by Karen Embry

Using the technique:

1. Refer to *General instructions—prepare* on pages 14–18. Prepare wood area to be painted.

2. Apply sealer to clock, following the manufacturer's instructions.

3. Using sponge, base-paint clock with Taffy. Let dry.

4. Enlarge Pieces of Time Pattern above. Transfer patchwork lines onto clock front.

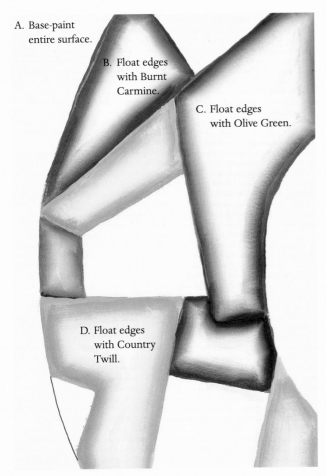

A. Base-paint entire surface.

B. Float edges with Burnt Carmine.

C. Float edges with Olive Green.

D. Float edges with Country Twill.

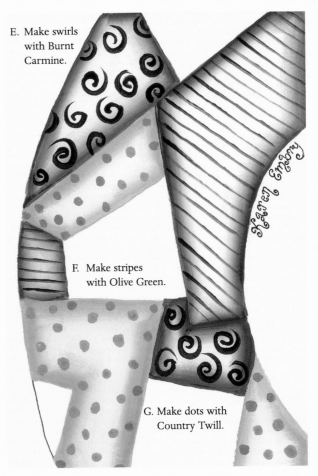

E. Make swirls with Burnt Carmine.

F. Make stripes with Olive Green.

G. Make dots with Country Twill.

5. Refer to *General instructions—paint design* on pages 19–22. Refer to Pieces of Time Painting Worksheets. Using angular, float outer edges of dotted sections with Country Twill. Using #4 liner, paint dots with Country Twill.

6. Using angular, float outer edges of swirled sections with Burnt Carmine. Using #4 liner, paint swirls with Burnt Carmine.

7. Using angular, float outer edges of striped sections with Olive Green. Using #1 liner, paint stripes with Olive Green.

8. Using round, paint rings around outside edge of clock with Pure Gold.

9. Float edges of clock's inner circle with Country Twill.

10. Transfer clock details onto clock center. Paint face details with Burnt Carmine. Let dry.

11. Refer to *General instructions—finish* on page 23. Sign project. Apply two coats of varnish, following manufacturer's instructions. Let dry.

12. Attach clockwork to clock.

9
technique

What you need to get started:

Painting surface:
Oval wooden tray, 16" x 8"

Acrylic craft paints:
Baby Pink
Hot Pink
Light Blue
Light Periwinkle
Rose White

Brushes:
Angular: ⅜"
Liner: #4
Round: #3
Scruffy
Wash: 1"

Additional supplies:
Aerosol finish, matte
Palette
Paper towel
Sandpaper
Tack cloth
Transfer tools
Water-based wood sealer

How do I dry-brush?

To dry-brush means to apply a small, almost dry, amount of paint to a dry surface to create a soft highlighted or shaded area.

Here's how:

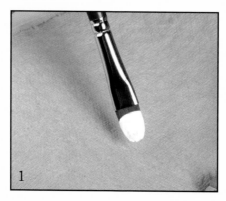

1. Using a round or filbert brush, dip bristles into paint puddle.

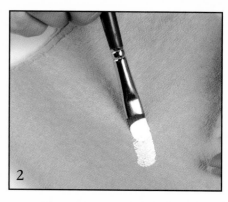

2. Blot excess paint on a paper towel.

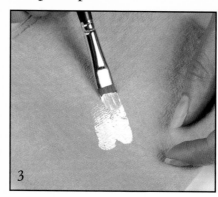

3. Brush back and forth to remove most of paint.

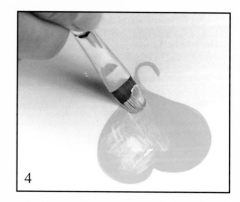

4. Touch bristles to desired area to be highlighted or shaded. Make a light circular motion, applying pressure where more paint is needed.

Sweetheart Tray

Designed by Karen Embry

Using the technique:

1. Refer to *General instructions—prepare* on pages 14–18. Prepare wood area to be painted.

2. Apply sealer to entire tray, following manufacturer's instructions.

3. Using wash brush, base-paint entire tray with Light Blue. Let dry.

4. Enlarge Heart Patterns on page 44 to fit center and sides of tray. Transfer patterns onto tray.

Heart Patterns

Repeat side design.

Enlarge 175%.

44

5. Refer to *General instructions—paint design* on pages 19–22. Refer to Heart Painting Worksheet. Using round, base-paint hearts with Baby Pink.

6. Using angular, float one side of each heart with Hot Pink.

7. Using scruffy, dry-brush unpainted side of each heart with Rose White.

8. Using liner, paint outer lines and dots with Rose White.

9. Using angular, float bottom inside edge of tray side with Light Periwinkle.

10. Paint top wavy line on tray side with Baby Pink. Paint bottom wavy line on tray side with Hot Pink.

11. Using handle end of brush, dot along wavy lines with Rose White. Let dry.

12. Refer to *General instructions—finish* on page 23. Sign project.

13. Apply two light coats of aerosol finish. Let dry between coats.

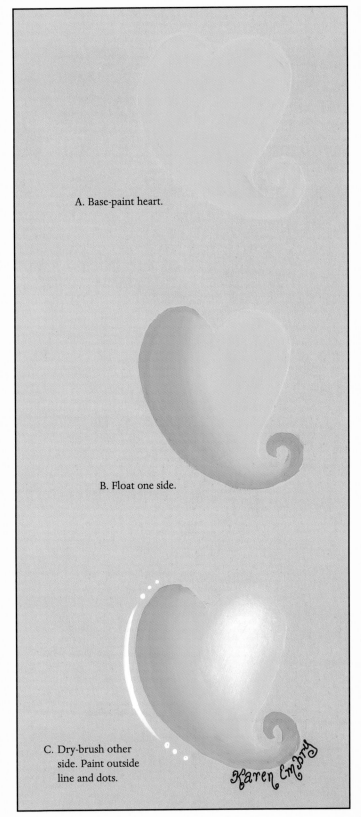

A. Base-paint heart.

B. Float one side.

C. Dry-brush other side. Paint outside line and dots.

Karen Embry

What you need to get started:

Painting surfaces:
Terra-cotta pots,
  4" dia. (2), 3" dia. (1)
Terra-cotta saucer, 8" dia. (1)
Wooden ball knob with flat
  side, ¾" dia.

Acrylic craft paints:
Heartland Blue
Licorice
Lipstick Red
Shamrock
Wicker White

Brushes:
Flats: #6, #10
Round: #1
Script liner: 18/0
Stencil: ¼"
Wash: ¾"

Additional supplies:
Aerosol finish, matte
Household sponge, 1" sq.
Industrial-strength craft glue
Palette
Paper towel
Pencil
Stylus
Transfer tools

How do I spatter?

The spattering technique is the manner of flecking paint onto a surface to obtain an antique look or to add color and character to a project.

Here's how:

1. Using stencil brush, dip bristles into water. Blot on paper towel to remove excess water. Dip bristle tips into paint. Work paint into bristles by tapping tips on palette.

2. Aim carefully at project and pull fingernail across bristles to release "spatters" of paint onto project.

Snowman Candy Dish

Designed by Susan Kelley

Using the technique:

1. Refer to *General instructions—prepare* on pages 14–18. Prepare terra-cotta and wood areas to be painted.

2. Stack all pots upside down temporarily to be certain they fit correctly. Stack one 4" pot directly on top of the other with rims touching. Rim of top 4" pot should fit snugly against rim of bottom 4" pot. Determine best fit and designate one for "top" and one for "bottom."

3. Using wash brush, base-paint top and rim of saucer, sides and bottom of 3" pot, and rim only of bottom pot with Lipstick Red. Base-paint sides of top pot with Wicker White.

4. Stack 3" pot onto top 4" pot. Using pencil, lightly mark on 4" pot where the 3" rim stops. Unstack pots.

5. Enlarge Snowman Patterns on page 48. Transfer scarf and hat patterns onto pots.

6. Refer to *General instructions—paint design* on pages 19–22. Refer to Snowman Painting Worksheet on page 49. Using wash brush, base-paint ball knob with Shamrock.

7. Using #6 flat, paint alternating stripes around rim of 3" pot with Heartland Blue and Shamrock.

8. Using round, underpaint squiggly lines with Wicker White. Let dry.

9. Overpaint lines with Lipstick Red.

10. Paint snowflake on side of hat with Wicker White. Using stylus, add dots.

11. Using #10 flat, paint scarf stripes with Heartland Blue, Lipstick Red, and Shamrock around rim of top 4" pot.

12. Using round, add snowflakes with Wicker White. Using stylus, add dots.

13. Turn pot upside down. Transfer face pattern onto pot.

14. Using stencil brush, dry-brush cheeks with Lipstick Red.

15. Using liner, paint eyes and mouth with Licorice. Paint candy cane nose with Wicker White.

16. Using round, add stripes with Lipstick Red.

17. Using liner, outline nose, brows, and lashes with thinned Licorice. For lashes keep brush up on bristle tips. Begin at eye and pull away in a light, sweeping motion.

18. Using stylus, dot eyes with Wicker White.

19. Using round, paint comma strokes at bottom of each eye.

20. Dampen sponge and squeeze out excess water. Dip sponge into Wicker White and add stripes around saucer rim. Let dry.

21. Refer to *General instructions—finish* on page 23. Using stencil brush, spatter complete project with Wicker White.

22. Turn pots upside down. Glue bottom pot into center of saucer. Glue top pot onto the bottom pot.

23. Apply glue inside rim of 3" pot and slide it over top pot. Glue ball knob into place.

24. Sign project. Apply two light coats of aerosol finish. Let dry between coats.

Snowman Patterns

Enlarge 220%.

Face

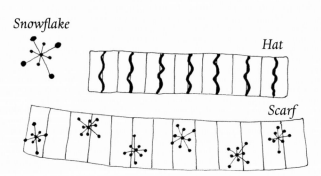

Snowflake

Hat

Scarf

Face:

A. Tap on cheek circles.

B. Paint mouth and eyes. Paint comma at bottom of each eye.

C. Dot eye centers. Paint candy cane stripes.

D. Outline facial features and add star.

Hat Cuff:

E. Undercoat cuff. Paint vertical stripes. Paint squiggly lines.

Scarf:

F. Paint vertical stripes. Paint snowflake lines. Dot ends of snowflake lines.

susan

What you need to get started:

Painting surfaces:

Slate with wooden frame, 12" x 9"

Acrylic craft paints:

Autumn Leaves
Burnt Umber
Buttercrunch
Clay Bisque
Country Twill
Grass Green
Hauser Green Dark
Licorice
Napthol Crimson
Nutmeg
Parchment
Slate Blue
Wicker White
Yellow Ochre

Brushes:

Angulars: ¼", ½"
Flats: #4, #6, #10, #12
Round: #1
Script liner: 18/0
Stencil: ¼"
Wash: ¾"

Additional supplies:

Aerosol finish, matte
Black craft wire, 18-gauge
Checkerboard stencil, ¼" or ⅜"
Power drill & small bit
Raffia
Wire cutters

How do I shade and highlight?

Shading creates shadows and a receding look while it darkens and deepens color. Highlighting adds dimension by adding light colors, making an area seem closer.

Here's how:

Shading:

1. Using a side-loaded brush, apply dark paint on slightly moistened surface.

Highlighting:

2. Using a side-loaded brush, apply light paint on slightly moistened surface.

Birdhouse Slate

Designed by Susan Kelley

Using the technique:

1. Refer to *General instructions—prepare* on pages 14–18. Prepare wood and slate areas to be painted.

2. Apply two coats of aerosol finish. Let dry between coats.

3. Using wash brush, base-paint slate and inside frame rim with Clay Bisque. Let dry.

4. Enlarge Birdhouse Patterns on page 52. Transfer patterns onto slate.

5. Using #12 flat, base-paint branch with Nutmeg.

6. Using #10 flat, base-paint birdhouse with Slate Blue. Base-paint birdie with Napthol Crimson.

7. Base-paint roof and border with Parchment.

8. Refer to *General instructions— paint design* on pages 19–22. Refer to Birdie & Vine Painting Worksheet on page 53. Using ½" angular, shade branch with Burnt Umber. Highlight with Clay Bisque. Let dry.

9. Transfer pattern details onto branch.

10. Using #6 flat, base-paint leaves with Hauser Green Dark. Highlight leaves with Grass Green.

11. Using round, paint stems with Grass Green. Shade stems with Hauser Green Dark.

12. Transfer pattern details onto birdhouse.

13. Using #4 flat, base-paint hole in roof with Nutmeg. Base-paint hanger with Buttercrunch.

14. Using ½" angular, shade birdhouse, roof, branch, and border with Burnt Umber.

15. Using #1 round, base-paint perch and opening with Burnt Umber. Highlight right side of opening with Clay Bisque.

16. Using round, paint and dot lettering on birdhouse with Parchment.

17. Transfer pattern details onto birdie.

18. Using ½" angular, shade birdie with Burnt Umber. Highlight with Autumn Leaves.

19. Using round, base-paint eyes with Licorice.

20. Using liner, paint eyelashes with thinned Licorice.

21. Using ¼" angular, highlight bottom eyes and dot with Wicker White.

22. Using #4 flat, base-paint beak with Yellow Ochre.

23. Using ¼" angular, shade beak with Burnt Umber. Shade edges of slate with Burnt Umber.

24. Using wash brush, base-paint frame with Country Twill.

25. Using stencil brush and stencil, paint checkers on frame with Parchment.

26. Transfer vine details onto frame.

27. Using liner, paint thinned Burnt Umber around frame and on birdhouse stripe. Paint some vines with thinned Hauser Green Dark. For birdie's vine, paint one vine with Hauser Green Dark.

28. Double-load #6 flat with Grass Green and Hauser Green Dark to paint all leaves.

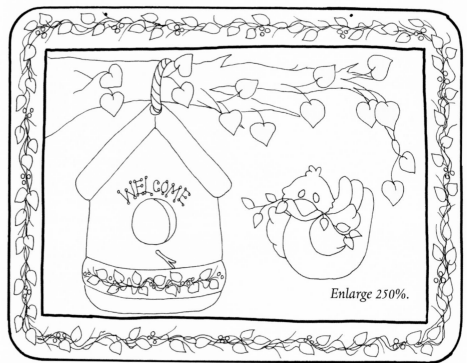

Enlarge 250%.

29. Using handle end of a brush, dot berries with Napthol Crimson.

30. Refer to *General instructions—finish* on page 23. Using stencil brush, spatter project with Burnt Umber, then with Parchment. Let dry.

31. Sign project. Apply two light coats of aerosol finish. Let dry between coats.

32. Drill two holes in the frame where indicated on pattern. Cut wire to curl and fit between drilled holes.

33. Thread wire through each hole for a hanger and curl ends.

34. Tie raffia bow onto wire hanger.

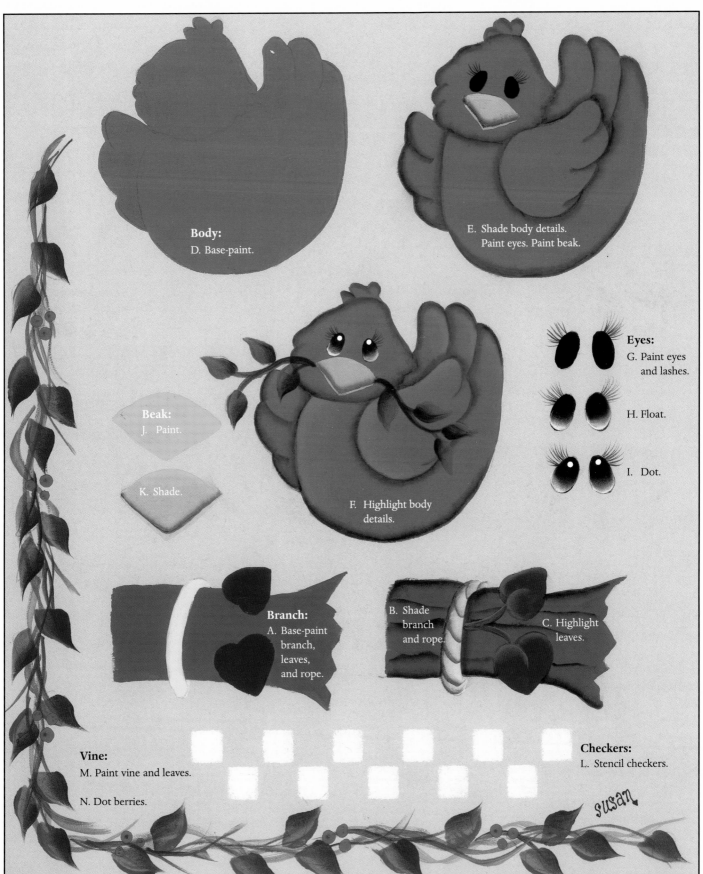

Birdie & Vine Painting Worksheet

Body:
D. Base-paint.

E. Shade body details.
Paint eyes. Paint beak.

Beak:
J. Paint.

K. Shade.

F. Highlight body details.

Eyes:
G. Paint eyes and lashes.

H. Float.

I. Dot.

Branch:
A. Base-paint branch, leaves, and rope.

B. Shade branch and rope.

C. Highlight leaves.

Vine:
M. Paint vine and leaves.

N. Dot berries.

Checkers:
L. Stencil checkers.

susan

What you need to get started:

Painting surface:
Wooden mantel clock,
   9" x 4½" x 1½"

Acrylic craft paints:
Burnt Umber
Buttercream
Dioxazine Purple
Grass Green
Ice Blue Dark
Licorice
Navy Blue
Purple Lilac
Raw Sienna
Thicket
Turner's Yellow
Violet Pansy
Wicker White

Brushes:
Angular: ¼"
Flats: #4, #6, #10
Liner: 10/0
Round: #1
Stencil 1"
Wash: ¾"

Additional supplies:
Aerosol finish, matte
Palette
Stylus
Transfer tools

How do I paint lettering?

Lettering can be painted freehand or written first with a pencil, then painted over.

Here's how:

1. Load liner with thinned paint. Holding brush perpendicular, balancing weight on wrist. Pull brush toward you while writing. Apply consistent pressure to keep letters uniform.

2. Using brush end, dot letter tips with paint.

Froggy's Time

Designed by Susan Kelley

Using the technique:

1. Refer to *General instructions—prepare* on pages 14–18. Remove clockwork. Prepare wood areas to be painted.

2. Using wash brush, base-paint clock with Buttercream. Let dry.

3. Enlarge Froggy's Time Pattern on page 56. Transfer pattern onto clock front.

4. Using #10 flat, base-paint frog with Grass Green.

5. Using #6 flat, base-paint lily pad with Thicket.

6. Using #10 flat, base-paint cattails with Raw Sienna. Let dry.

7. Transfer pattern details onto clock front.

8. Refer to *General instructions—paint design* on pages 19–22. Refer to Frog, Dragonflies & Cattails Painting Worksheet on page 57.

9. Using angular, shade around body details of frog with Thicket.

10. Using stylus, dot body with Turner's Yellow.

11. Paint eyes with Wicker White. Let dry. Dot irises with Licorice.

12. Using angular, highlight lily pad with Buttercream.

13. Using chiseled edge of #4 flat, pull grass blades up from bottom of clock with Grass Green.

14. Using angular, shade grass with Thicket.

15. Using liner, highlight blades of grass with Wicker White.

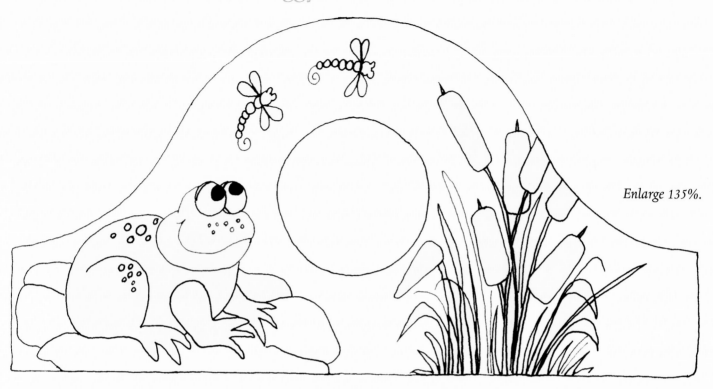

Enlarge 135%.

16. Dry-brush cattails with Buttercream.

17. Shade cattails and add tips with Burnt Umber.

18. Using handle end of brush, dot dragonflies' bodies with Violet Pansy.

19. Using liner, paint dragonflies' tails with Dioxazine Purple.

20. Using round, paint dragonflies' wings with Wicker White.

21. Using angular, highlight dragonflies with Purple Lilac. Shade with Dioxazine Purple.

22. Shade wings with Navy Blue.

23. Using round, paint lettering with thinned Grass Green.

24. Using angular, shade outer edges of clock front with Ice Blue Dark.

25. Using stencil brush, spatter project with Thicket. Let dry.

26. Refer to *General instructions—finish* on page 23. Sign project.

27. Apply two light coats of aerosol finish. Let dry between coats.

28. Replace clockwork.

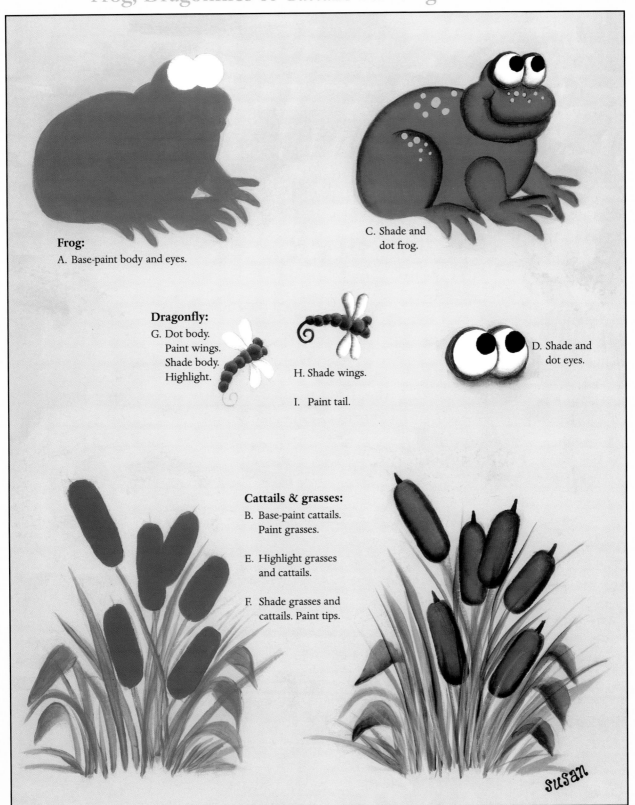

Frog:

A. Base-paint body and eyes.

C. Shade and dot frog.

Dragonfly:

G. Dot body.
Paint wings.
Shade body.
Highlight.

H. Shade wings.

I. Paint tail.

D. Shade and dot eyes.

Cattails & grasses:

B. Base-paint cattails.
Paint grasses.

E. Highlight grasses and cattails.

F. Shade grasses and cattails. Paint tips.

susan

What you need to get started:

Painting surface:
Ivory pillar candle, 3" dia. (6" tall)
Terra-cotta pot & saucer, 4"

Acrylic craft paints:
Burnt Umber
Buttercream
Dioxazine Purple
Grass Green
Ice Blue Dark
Licorice
Navy Blue
Purple Lilac
Raw Sienna
Thicket
Turner's Yellow
Violet Pansy
Wicker White

Brushes:
Angular: ⅛"
Flats: #6, #10
Liner: 10/0
Round: #1
Stencil
Wash: ¼"

Other supplies:
Aerosol finish, matte
Craft glue
Glass & tile medium
Sea sponge

How do I paint on wax surfaces?

Acrylic paints tend to bead up when they are applied to waxy surfaces, and peel away when they are dry. Using a glass and tile medium can help you create lovely, lasting wax-based pieces.

Here's how:

1. Apply a glass and tile medium, or give it a light spray of matte acrylic sealer. *Note: This will give the surface some "tooth" so the paint does not bead up.*

2. After paint is applied and dry, spray with matte sealer or apply medium again.

Frog & Cattails Candleholder

Designed by Susan Kelley

Using the technique:

1. Refer to *General instructions—prepare* on pages 14–18. Prepare terra-cotta areas to be painted.

2. Using wash brush, base-paint pot and saucer with Buttercream. Let dry.

3. Using dampened sponge, pat pot rims and saucer with Ice Blue Dark. Let dry.

4. Transfer Frog Pattern on page 61 onto pot.

5. Base-paint frog with Grass Green.

6. Using handle end of brush, dot dragonflies' bodies with Violet Pansy.

7. Refer to *General instructions—paint design* on pages 19–22. Refer to Frog, Dragonflies & Cattails Painting Worksheet on page 57. Using angular, shade frog with Thicket.

8. Using #6 flat, base-paint eyes with Wicker White. Let dry.

9. Dot eyes with Licorice. Let dry.

10. Dot eyes with Wicker White. Dot nose area with Turner's Yellow.

11. Using liner, paint mouth with Licorice.

12. Using liner, paint dragonflies' tails with Dioxazine Purple.

13. Using round, paint dragonflies' wings with Wicker White.

14. Using angular, shade dragonflies with Dioxazine Purple.

15. Highlight with Purple Lilac.

16. Shade wings with Navy Blue.

17. Refer to *General instructions—finish* on page 23. Using stencil brush, spatter project with Thicket. Let dry.

18. Turn pot upside down and glue saucer to top (previously bottom) of pot.

19. Apply two light coats of aerosol finish. Let dry between coats.

Frog & Cattails Candle

1. Using wash brush, paint candle with glass and tile medium. Let dry.

2. Using dampened sponge, pat randomly around candle with Buttercream.

3. Using wash brush, float Ice Blue Dark around top edge of candle. Let dry.

4. Transfer Cattails Pattern on page 61 onto candle.

5. Refer to Frog, Dragonflies & Cattails Painting Worksheet on page 57. Using chiseled edge of #6 flat, paint grass with Grass Green.

6. Base-paint cattails with Raw Sienna.

7. Using #10 flat, shade grass with Thicket.

8. Dry-brush cattail highlights with Buttercream.

9. Using angular, highlight grass with Buttercream.

10. Shade cattails and paint tips with Burnt Umber. Let dry.

11. Refer to *General instructions—finish* on page 23. Using stencil brush, spatter candle with Thicket. Let dry.

12. Sign project.

13. Apply two light coats of aerosol finish. Let dry between coats.

14. Place candle into candleholder.

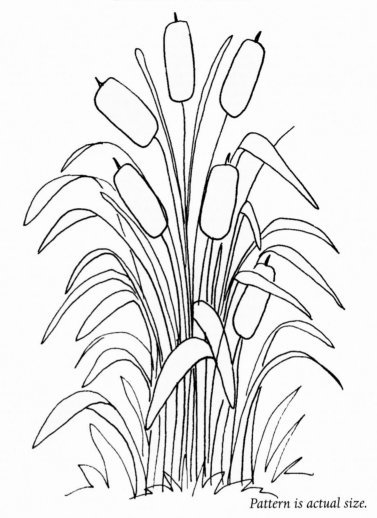

Pattern is actual size.

Frog Pattern

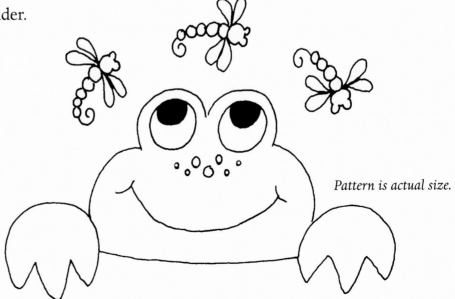

Pattern is actual size.

14
technique

What you need to get started:

Painting surface:
Decorative wooden signboard,
14" x 4"

Acrylic craft paints:
Clover
Coastal Blue
Engine Red
Fawn
Honeycomb
Inca Gold (Metallic)
Light Blue
Linen
Pure Black
Pure Orange
Titanium White

Brushes:
Angular: ⅜"
Liner: #2
Rounds: #1, #3
Wash: 1"

Additional supplies:
¼" screw eyes, 1" long (2)
Aerosol finish, matte
Black permanent marker,
    ultrafine-point
Cosmetic blush, frosted pink
Cotton swab
Palette knife
Ribbon, 1 yd.

How do I mix colors?

Colors can be lightened or darkened, or a new color formed when paints are mixed together.

Here's how:

1. Squeeze colors to be mixed on palette.

2. Using palette knife, bring the colors together in a puddle. *Note: Always add lighter color to darker.*

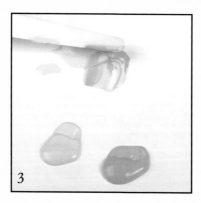

3. Mix paints together, creating a third color. Add lighter color as needed to obtain desired shade.

4. Mix paints together well on palette.

Snowman & Globe Sign

Designed by Karen Embry

Using the technique:

1. Refer to *General instructions—prepare* on pages 14–18. Prepare wood area to be painted.

2. Using wash brush, base-paint signboard with Fawn. Let dry.

3. Enlarge Snowman & Globe Pattern on page 64. Transfer pattern onto signboard.

4. Refer to *General instructions—paint design* on pages 19–22. Refer to Snowman & Globe Painting Worksheet on page 65. Using #3 round, base-paint snowman with Titanium White.

5. Using angular, float right side of snowman with Light Blue.

6. Transfer pattern details for face and buttons onto signboard.

7. Using #1 round, base-paint nose with Pure Orange.

Enlarge 300%

8. Float bottom of nose with Engine Red.

9. Paint arms with Honeycomb.

10. Highlight along top of arms with Linen.

11. Paint buttons with Pure Black.

12. Using #3 round, base-paint globe with Light Blue plus Coastal Blue (1:1).

13. Using #1 round, paint land with Clover.

14. Using liner, paint stars with Light Blue.

15. Paint lettering and the trim along upper and lower edges of signboard with Inca Gold.

16. Refer to *General instructions—finish* on page 23. Using marker, draw facial details.

17. Using cotton swab, apply blush to cheeks.

18. Sign project.

19. Attach two screw eyes into top edge of signboard about 1" from sides.

20. Apply two light coats of aerosol finish. Let dry between coats.

21. Tie ribbon to screw eyes for a hanger.

A. Base-paint snowman. Float left-hand side of snowman.

B. Base-paint globe, nose, arms, buttons.

C. Float bottom edge of nose.

D. Highlight tops of arms.

E. Paint land part of globe.

F. Draw eyes, brows, and mouth.

G. Rub on cheeks.

Karen Embry

15 technique

Stippling, also known as "pouncing," is used to achieve a slightly rough look such as fur, sand, or the illusion of greenery in a landscape painting.

What you need to get started:

Painting surface:
Wooden plate, 9½" dia.

Acrylic craft paints:
Burnt Umber
Dove Gray
Licorice
Light Blue
Linen
Medium Gray
Raw Sienna
Sunflower
Titanium White
Turner's Yellow
Warm White

Brushes:
Angulars: ¼", ½"
Deerfoot: ⅜"
Filbert: #8
Script liner: 20/0

Additional supplies:
Brush-on water-based varnish, matte
Cloth
Cosmetic sponge
Palette
Sandpaper
Tack cloth
Transfer tools
Water-based wood varnish

Here's how:

1. Dip a dry deerfoot into desired paint on palette.

2. Stroke brush back and forth to load paint into bristles.

3. On a clean area of the palette, pounce brush up and down to remove excess paint.

4. Apply to project when desired look is achieved. Wipe stippler with a cloth to clean between colors. Do not wash stippler until you are finished for the day. You cannot stipple with a damp brush.

Honey Bear Plate

Designed by Laraine Short

Using the technique:

1. Refer to *General instructions—prepare* on pages 14–18. Prepare wood area to be painted.

2. Apply sealer, following manufacturer's instructions. Let dry. Sand. Using tack cloth, wipe clean.

3. Using sponge, paint inside plate with Warm White and rim with Light Blue. Let dry.

4. Enlarge Honey Bear Pattern on page 68. Transfer outside lines of pattern items onto plate center.

5. Using filbert, base-paint bear with Raw Sienna.

6. Base-paint spoon with Medium Gray.

7. Base-paint bees' bodies, the hive, and the honey with Turner's Yellow.

8. Refer to *General instructions—paint design* on pages 19–22. Refer to Bear & Hive Painting Worksheet on page 69. Transfer all pattern details onto plate.

9. Using stippler, shade appropriate areas of bear with Burnt Umber.

10. Stipple bear highlights with Sunflower. Let dry.

11. Using liner, paint bear facial features with inky Licorice.

12. Highlight eyes with Titanium White.

13. Paint lines on nose with inky Dove Gray.

14. Using ½" angular, shade under bear with Linen.

15. Using stippler, shade hive with Raw Sienna. Highlight with Sunflower.

16. Using ¼" angular, shade spoon with Licorice. Highlight with Dove Gray.

17. Using ¼" angular, shade honey on spoon with Raw Sienna. Highlight with Sunflower.

18. Highlight bees' bodies with Sunflower.

19. Base-paint the wings with Titanium White. Shade with Medium Gray.

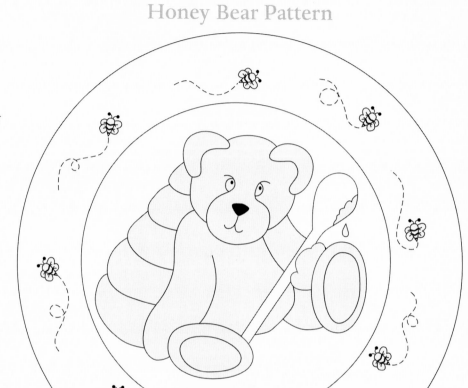

Honey Bear Pattern

Enlarge 225%.

20. Using liner, paint stripes, stingers, and antennae with inky Licorice. Pull lines on wings out from body. Paint "flight lines" behind bees.

21. Refer to *General instructions—finish* on page 23. Sign project.

22. Apply two coats of varnish, following manufacturer's instructions. Let dry.

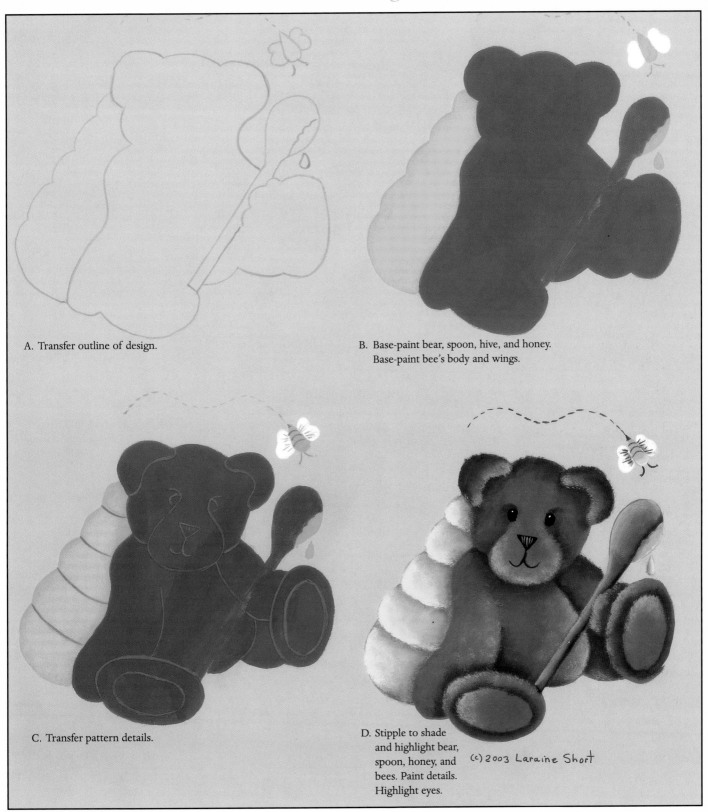

A. Transfer outline of design.

B. Base-paint bear, spoon, hive, and honey.
   Base-paint bee's body and wings.

C. Transfer pattern details.

D. Stipple to shade
   and highlight bear,
   spoon, honey, and
   bees. Paint details.
   Highlight eyes.

(c) 2003 Laraine Short

How do I multiload?

What you need to get started:

Painting surface:
Small scalloped metal tray

Acrylic craft paints:
Cobalt Blue
Dark Night
Dioxazine Purple
Dove Gray
Night Sky
Old Ivy
Orange Light
Periwinkle
Pure Black
Sage Green
Warm White

Brushes:
Flats: #2, #4, #6
Liner: #10/0
Round: #2
Stencil roller: 1"

Additional supplies:
Aerosol metal primer
Blending gel medium
Brush-on water-based varnish, satin
Palette
Paper towel
Sandpaper, fine-grit
Tack cloth
Transfer tools

Many colors can be painted at one time when brush is multiloaded. This technique is used to shade and highlight.

Here's how:

1. Load side of brush with one paint color.

2. Double-load brush in different paint color.

3. Stroke back and forth to blend paints.

4. Dip corner of brush into a third color.

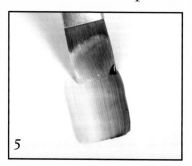

5. Stroke brush to blend and distribute color.

6. Paint each design with a single stroke.

technique 17:
What is a dirty brush?

A dirty brush contains wet paint left in the brush from the last application. Gently wipe excess paint onto a paper towel before picking up the next color. This provides a hint of the previous color along with the new color.

Shades of Blue

Designed by Mary McCullah

Using the techniques:

1. Refer to *General instructions—prepare* on pages 14–18. Prepare metal area to be painted. Prime with aerosol metal primer.

2. Using roller, base-paint entire tray, with Dove Gray plus Periwinkle (3:1). Let dry.

3. Enlarge Shades of Blue Patterns on page 73 to fit tray. Transfer patterns onto tray.

4. Refer to *General instructions—paint design* on pages 19–22. Refer to Shades of Blue Painting Worksheet on page 75. Using liner, unevenly fill outside edge of all four butterfly wings with Dove Gray.

5. Using #4 flat and starting at top of left-top wing section, base-paint each wing section with Periwinkle.

6. About ⅔ of the way down the wing, pick up a touch of Dioxazine Purple, blending it into the dirty brush. Fill in bottom section of the wings with mixture. Repeat process for other three wing sections.

7. Using #2 flat, mix Dark Night plus a touch of Pure Black. Paint mixture on left side of body and fill in head.

8. Using liner, pull Dove Gray from right side of body to left for highlight.

9. Using #6 flat, place a thin wash of Cobalt Blue plus blending gel over each wing section, except the light edge.

10. Using liner, lighten edges of wings with Warm White, leaving an uneven edge. Let dry.

11. Paint in the dark areas on wings with Pure Black. Paint division lines with Pure Black.

12. Tap markings on bottom wing sections with Orange Light.

13. Double-load flats, depending on size of hydrangeas petal, with Dove Gray on one side and Cobalt Blue on other. While blending on palette, add a touch of Night Sky or Dioxazine Purple to darker side for variety. *Note: Picking up a little blending gel as you load the brush will make it easier to paint the petals.*

14. Once brush is loaded, pull brush across petal with light color to outside edge. Wiggle brush a little to leave soft brush stroke marks.

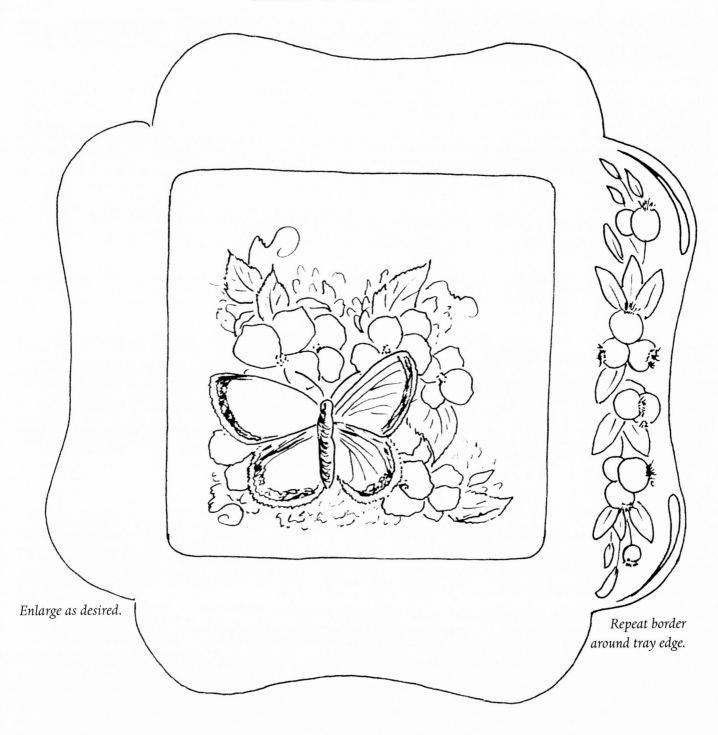

Enlarge as desired.

Repeat border around tray edge.

15. Using flats, shade on main blossoms with a float of Cobalt Blue on bluer toned petals and Night Sky for a lavender accent.

16. Lighten outer edges with Warm White.

17. Using liner, tap Orange Light centers on main blossoms.

18. Once main petals are completed, add some soft, indistinct petals under butterfly and around main flower petals. Use very little color on the brush. Use some Cobalt Blue and Sage Green multiloaded with Dove Gray for "illusive" petals.

19. Use #2 and #4 flats to fill in leaves. Base-paint light leaves with Sage Green. Fill in darker leaves with Sage Green plus a touch of Old Ivy.

20. Using flats, float on shading. Use Old Ivy for lighter value leaves, and Old Ivy plus Night Sky for darker leaves.

21. Using liner, make vein lines with thinned Old Ivy plus Night Sky.

22. Using a side-loaded brush, accent with Orange Light.

23. Using #2 flat, base-paint berries with a mixture of Cobalt Blue plus Dark Night.

24. Alter ratio of this mixture so berries will be slightly different in color and value. Add a touch of Sage Green to small berries.

25. Using #4 flat, shade to further separate berries with mixture of Cobalt Blue plus Night Sky on lightest berries, Night Sky on some medium value areas, and Night Sky plus Pure Black on darkest areas. *Note: More than one layer may be necessary.*

26. Highlight with Warm White. Let dry.

27. Dry-brush lightest areas with Warm White.

28. Using liner, pull out thin lines on blossom end with Night Sky plus Pure Black.

29. Paint thin lines of Pure Black for butterfly antennae.

30. Paint stems in the border and squiggly lines in blossom area with Old Ivy.

31. Using #2 round, paint comma strokes on edges of tray with Cobalt tipped in Night Sky. Practice on the palette for desired stroke.

32. Using #6 flat, paint inside border with two coats of Night Sky. Let dry between coats.

33. Refer to *General instructions—finish* on page 23. Sign project.

34. Apply varnish, following manufacturer's instructions. Let dry.

Butterfly:
A. Base-paint wings
   and body.

B. Highlight wings
   and edges.

Berries:
G. Base-paint berries
   and leaves.

Hydrangea:
C. Base-paint blossoms.

D. Highlight blossoms.
   Shade blossom centers.

H. Shade and
   highlight berries
   and leaves.
   Accent leaves.

Leaves:
E. Base-paint leaves.

F. Shade and highlight leaves.
   Accent vein lines.

Section 3: Beyond the basics

Objects can look shaded merely by strategically placing a darker color next to a lighter color. It is all in the placement and the neatness of the painting.

What you need to get started:

Painting surfaces:
Wooden ball knob, 1½" dia.
Wooden box & lid
    5½" sq. x 2½" high

Acrylic craft paints:
Camel
Clover
French Vanilla
Lime Yellow
Peach Perfection
Pure Gold (Metallic)
Rose Garden
Wicker White

Brushes:
Angular: ½"
Rounds: #1, #4
Script liner: 2/0
Wash: 1"

Additional supplies:
Aerosol finish, matte
Craft glue
Palette
Sandpaper
Stylus
Tack cloth
Transfer tools
Water-based wood sealer

Here's how:

1. Depending on the width of the desired line, use a liner, round brush, or scroller.

2. Hold brush perpendicular to the surface while stroking darker color onto one side of the design element.

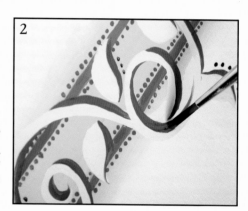

Decorative Vine Box

Designed by Karen Embry

Using the technique:

1. Refer to *General instructions—prepare* on pages 14–18. Prepare wood areas to be painted. Apply sealer, following manufacturer's instructions.

2. Using wash brush, base-paint box and lid with French Vanilla. Let dry.

3. Transfer Decorative Vine Patterns on page 80 onto box and lid.

4. Refer to *General instructions—paint design* on pages 19–22. Refer to Decorative Vine Painting Worksheet on page 81. Using wash brush, paint bands diagonally across lid and horizontally around box with Peach Perfection plus a touch of Wicker White.

5. Using #1 round, paint thin lines at edges of bands with Rose Garden.

6. Using angular, float outside edges of bands with Camel.

7. Using stylus, paint tiny dots near edges of bands with Rose Garden.

8. Transfer pattern details onto box and lid.

9. Using #4 round, paint vine and leaves with Lime Yellow.

10. Using #1 round, paint darker vine areas and leaf accents with Clover.

11. Using liner, paint tiny dots around the vines and leaves with Clover.

12. Using #4 round, paint trim around lid and knob with Pure Gold. Let dry.

13. Refer to *General instructions— finish* on page 23. Center and glue knob onto lid.

14. Sign project.

15. Apply two coats of aerosol finish. Let dry between each coat.

Decorative Vine Patterns

Side

Patterns are actual size.

Lid

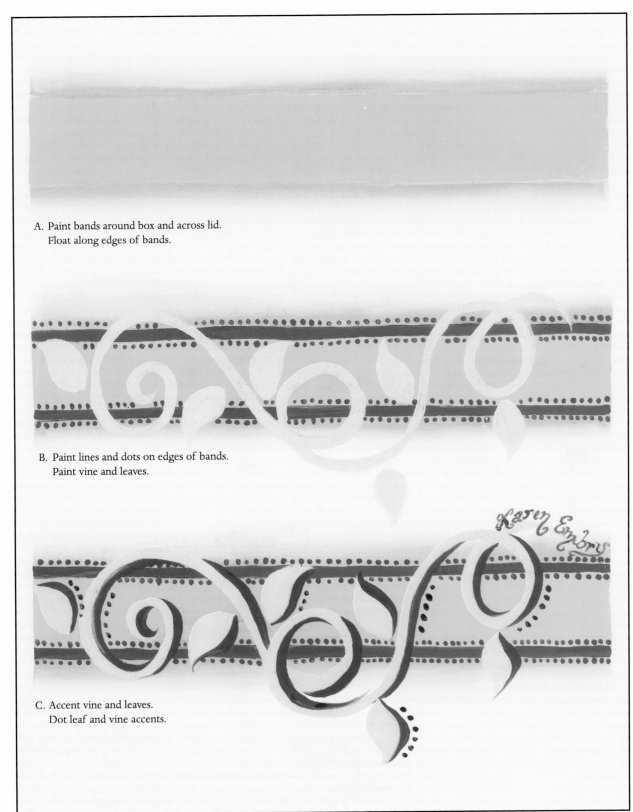

A. Paint bands around box and across lid.
   Float along edges of bands.

B. Paint lines and dots on edges of bands.
   Paint vine and leaves.

C. Accent vine and leaves.
   Dot leaf and vine accents.

2

project

What you need to get started:

Painting surfaces:
Dark green plastic heart-shaped box & lid, approx. 7½" dia.

Paints for plastics:
Black
Bright Red
Brown
Hunter Green
Light Pink
Turquoise
White
Yellow

Brushes:
Angular: ½"
Filbert: #8
Flat: #6
Mop
Script liner: 20/0

Additional supplies:
Blow dryer
Cosmetic sponge
Extender
Palette
Transfer tools

How do I use extender and a mop brush?

A soft blended look is acquired by using a mop brush. Extender lengthens the drying time of the paint, giving you the extra time to manipulate it.

Here's how:

1. Using clean dry brush, apply extender to painted areas. Leave no puddles.

2. Using angular, shade design with a darker color.

3. Using clean dry mop, pat to blend and soften. Using blow dryer, dry extender.

4. Using "extender" brush, reapply extender. Using angular, highlight design.

5. Using clean dry mop, pat to blend and soften. Using blow dryer, dry extender.

Pink Heart Box

Designed by Laraine Short

Using the technique:

1. Refer to *General instructions—prepare* on pages 14–18. Prepare plastic area to be painted.

2. Using sponge, base-paint box and lid with Hunter Green. Let dry.

3. Transfer Pink Flower Pattern onto lid.

4. Refer to *General instructions—paint design* on pages 19–22. Refer to Pink Flower Painting Worksheet on page 85. Using filbert, base paint petals with Light Pink. Base-paint centers with Brown. Let dry.

5. Using a clean dry brush, add extender to painted areas.

6. Using angular, shade one side of petals with Bright Red. Using mop, pat to blend and soften. Let dry.

7. Using "extender" brush, reapply extender to painted areas.

8. Using angular, highlight the remaining sides of the petals with White. Using mop, pat to blend and soften. Let dry.

9. Using angular, shade center with Black. Dab center with a mixture of Yellow plus White (1:1) to lighten.

10. Using liner, pull lines out from center with thinned Black.

11. Using filbert, base-paint leaves with a mixture of Hunter Green plus White (1:1).

12. Using angular, shade with Hunter Green.

13. Highlight with a mixture of Hunter Green plus White (1:2).

Pink Flower Pattern

Pattern is actual size.

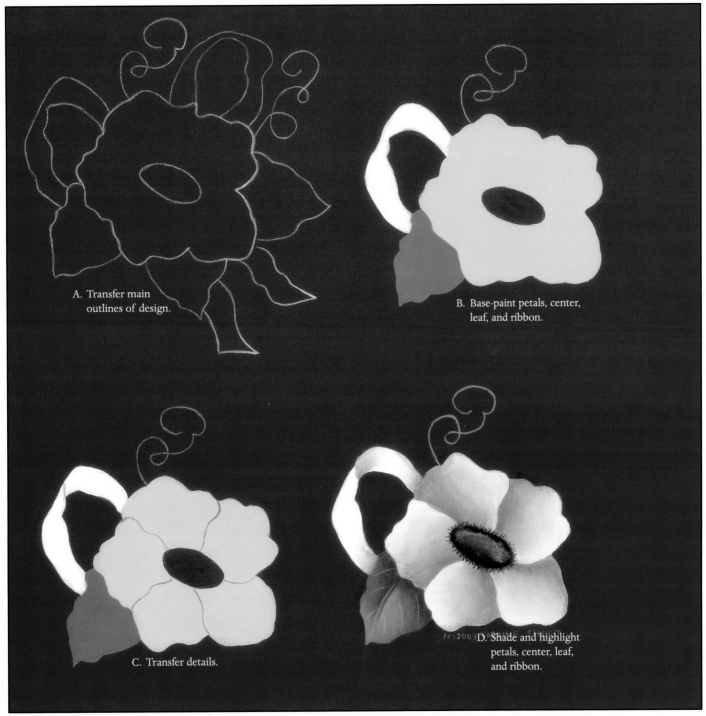

A. Transfer main outlines of design.

B. Base-paint petals, center, leaf, and ribbon.

C. Transfer details.

D. Shade and highlight petals, center, leaf, and ribbon.

14. Using liner, paint veins and tendrils with a mixture of Hunter Green plus White (1:2).

15. Using filbert, base-paint ribbon with White.

16. Using angular, shade ribbon with Turquoise. Let dry.

17. Refer to *General instructions—finish* on page 23. Sign project.

3
project

What you need to get started:

Painting surfaces:
Oval frame with 5" x 9" opening Masonite, wood, or canvas background surface, cut to fit oval frame opening

Acrylic craft paints:
Clover
Green Umber
Hauser Green Light
Hauser Green Medium
Pure Magenta
Turner's Yellow
Warm White

Brushes:
Filbert: #4
Flats: #4, #10, #12
Liner: #1
Wash: ¾"

Additional supplies:
Blending gel medium
Brush-on water-based varnish, satin
Clean water
Cloth
Glazing medium
Palette
Sandpaper
Sea sponge
Tack cloth
Transfer tools

How can a brush stroke create different effects?

A single stroke of the brush can create a flower petal. This project shows three or four single brush strokes combined to make lovely wild-flowers. The leaves require additional colors for shading and highlighting.

Here's how:

1. Load or double-load brush. Pull brush toward center of design. Be certain to connect lines in the center. This will leave a smooth outer stroke while the inside can be covered by the painted center.

Wildflowers Frame

Designed by Priscilla Hauser

Using the technique:

1. Refer to *General instructions—prepare* on pages 14–18. Prepare wood and background areas to be painted.

2. Using wash brush, base-paint frame with Warm White. Let dry.

3. Sand edges of frame to remove some paint to achieve a worn look.

4. Dip sponge in clean water and squeeze out any excess.

5. Dip sponge in Green Umber. Blot on cloth. Dip in glazing medium. Blot on cloth. In a dabbing motion, apply paint to background.

6. While paint is still wet, dip sponge in glazing medium, blot on rag, and pick up Hauser Green Light. Blend Hauser Green Light into Green Umber. *Note: More Green Umber, more glazing medium, and more Hauser Green Light may be added—you want a light, airy background.* Let dry.

7. Transfer Wildflowers Pattern on page 89 onto background surface.

8. Refer to *General instructions—paint design* on pages 19–22. Refer to Wildflowers Painting Worksheet on page 90. Using #10 flat, base-paint leaves with Clover. Let dry.

9. Using #12 flat, float Green Umber shading at base of leaves and where one leaf overlaps another. Start at background of design and move forward, painting one leaf at a time. Let dry. *Note: Leaves toward the back of the design are darker, and leaves toward the front are lighter.*

10. Using #10 flat, apply blending gel to leaf.

11. Using #12 flat, shade with Green Umber.

12. Highlight with Hauser Green Light plus Warm White. Wipe brush, and blend from top to bottom and bottom to top. Do not overblend or overwork leaf.

13. Mix a light magenta color with Pure Magenta plus Warm White (2:3). *Note: Front flowers are painted lighter than back flowers. To achieve this, add more Warm White.*

14. Using filbert, paint four strokes with inky magenta mixture. Start at outside edge, then press and lift slightly while drawing into center. *Notes: A second or third coat may be needed to cover. For smaller flowers, use smaller brush.*

15. Using liner, paint fine lines from center out onto each petal with thinned Pure Magenta. Let dry.

16. Paint some thin white lines from center out onto petals with thinned Warm White.

17. Add a dot of Turner's Yellow to center.

18. Paint buds as shown on worksheet.

19. Paint stems with Hauser Green Medium. Shade with Green Umber. Highlight with Warm White.

20. Paint calyxes with Clover. Shade with Green Umber.

21. Using #4 flat, float mixture of Pure Magenta plus Green Umber (1:1) at base of each leaf. Let dry.

22. Apply blending gel and above mixture on shadows. Wipe brush on cloth and blend.

23. Using liner, create stems with thinned mixture. Let dry.

24. Refer to *General instructions— finish* on page 23. Sign project.

25. Apply two coats of varnish, following manufacturer's instructions. Let project dry between coats.

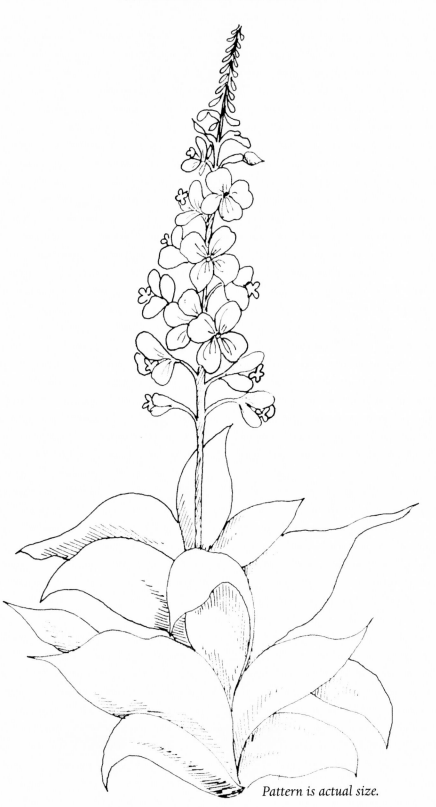

Pattern is actual size.

Wildflowers Painting Worksheet

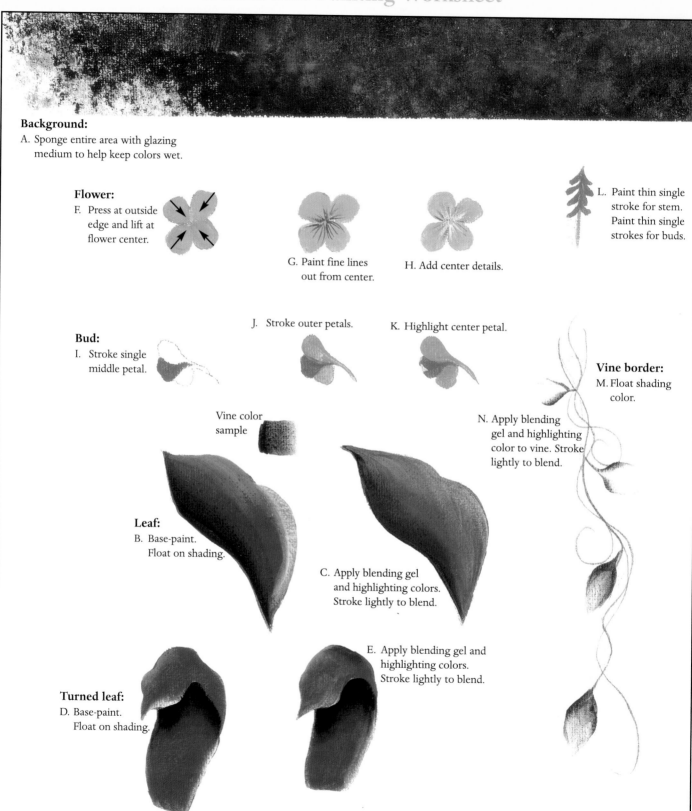

Background:
A. Sponge entire area with glazing medium to help keep colors wet.

Flower:
F. Press at outside edge and lift at flower center.

G. Paint fine lines out from center.

H. Add center details.

L. Paint thin single stroke for stem. Paint thin single strokes for buds.

Bud:
I. Stroke single middle petal.

J. Stroke outer petals.

K. Highlight center petal.

Vine border:
M. Float shading color.

N. Apply blending gel and highlighting color to vine. Stroke lightly to blend.

Vine color sample

Leaf:
B. Base-paint. Float on shading.

C. Apply blending gel and highlighting colors. Stroke lightly to blend.

E. Apply blending gel and highlighting colors. Stroke lightly to blend.

Turned leaf:
D. Base-paint. Float on shading.

How can I paint on a crackled finish?

To give an aged look, different degrees of crackling can be achieved from subtle to bold, depending on the heaviness of the topcoat. Additionally, crackle medium will react differently when it is applied with a sponge than with a brush.

Here's how:

1. Base-paint project with acrylic paint. Let dry.

2. Using sponge brush, apply generous coat of crackle medium. Let dry.

3. Apply a clear or colored acrylic topcoat. As it dries, the cracks will form. *Note: A thick topcoat produces large cracks. A thin topcoat produces smaller cracks.*

Tips:

- Practice on test surface before working on project.

- Avoid restroking over areas while adding topcoat or cracks may diminish.

- Do not dry paint with blow dryer when crackling.

- A small amount of water added to topcoat paint gives a fine web of crackling.

- Low humidity enhances crackling.

What you need to get started:

Painting surface:
Pine board, 11¼" x 19"

Acrylic craft paints:
Asphaltum
Burnt Sienna
Burnt Umber
Lemonade
Prussian Blue
Pure Magenta
Rose Pink
Teal Green
Thicket
Titanium White
Warm White

Brushes:
Filbert: #6
Flats: #10, ¼"
Round: #3
Small scruffy
Sponge

Additional supplies:
Aerosol finish, matte
Crackle medium
Floating medium
Paper towel
Sandpaper, fine-grit
Sea sponge
Tack cloth
Water-based wood sealer

How do I tint?

Tinting is used to subtly add contrasting color for interest and depth in the design.

Here's how:

1. Load a small amount of contrasting paint on a filbert brush and apply to the project. To soften the color, lightly brush with a mop brush to blend out the tint.

Topiary Painting

Designed by Donna Lee Parella

Using the techniques:

1. Refer to *General instructions—prepare* on pages 14–18. Prepare wood area to be painted. Apply wood sealer. Let dry.

2. Lightly sand rough spots. Remove dust with tack cloth. Using sponge brush, base-paint board with Asphaltum. Let dry.

3. Apply a thin coat of crackle medium, following manufacturer's instructions. Let dry.

4. Using ¾" flat and long, even strokes, top-coat with Warm White. *Note: Be careful not to stroke over same area twice.* Let dry.

5. Apply sealer, following manufacturer's instructions. Let dry.

6. Enlarge Topiary Pattern on page 94. Transfer pattern onto board.

7. Refer to *General instructions—paint design* on pages 19–22. Refer to Topiary Painting Worksheet on page 95. Using sea sponge, pounce hydrangea background with Pure Magenta.

8. Double-load filbert with Pure Magenta and small amount of Titanium White. Paint petals in clusters of one, two, three, and four, starting from bottom of hydrangea. For more contrast, add Rose Pink to brush plus Pure Magenta while stroking petals.

9. At center-top point of hydrangea, load more Titanium White to brush along with Pure Magenta. Create open four-petal clusters at center-top point. Highlight them generously. *Note: If the brush becomes too "muddy," wash or wipe it out and reload.*

10. Using handle end of small brush, dot four-petal-cluster centers with Lemonade.

11. Multiload ¾" flat with Teal Green, Titanium White, and floating medium. *Note: The pot and leaves stay transparent when using floating medium, adding to the beauty by allowing crackle*

background to show through. Start stroke on chiseled edge at top outer edge of pot, keeping darker value to the outside. At bottom of pot, push down vertically and lift to chiseled edge of brush.

12. At about center of pot, stop and start at opposite outer edge of pot, keeping darker value at outer edge giving pot a rounded appearance.

13. To create lip on pot, pull in a horizontal stroke across top.

14. Load damp #10 flat with Teal Green plus a touch of Prussian Blue. Paint horizontal strokes at bottom point of pot.

15. Repeat strokes with Pure Magenta plus Thicket. Alternate shades, creating softer strokes as they fade.

16. Double-load round with Burnt Sienna and Burnt Umber. Paint trunk, keeping darker value at outer edge of both sides.

17. Wipe brush on paper towel, then add Titanium White. Highlight face of trunk.

18. Multiload #10 flat with Teal Green, Thicket, and floating medium. Blend mixture on palette, keeping it transparent.

19. Paint leaves, keeping Thicket to outer edge and Teal Green to center. Let dry.

20. Using filbert, tint leaves with Pure Magenta plus floating medium.

21. Double-load scruffy with Lemonade and Thicket. Pounce in greens. Pounce in high lights with Titanium White. Let dry.

22. Refer to *General instructions—finish* on page 23. Sign project.

23. Apply two light coats of aerosol finish. Let dry between coats.

Topiary Pattern

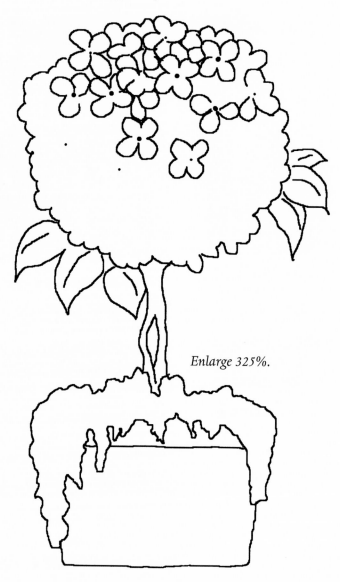

Enlarge 325%.

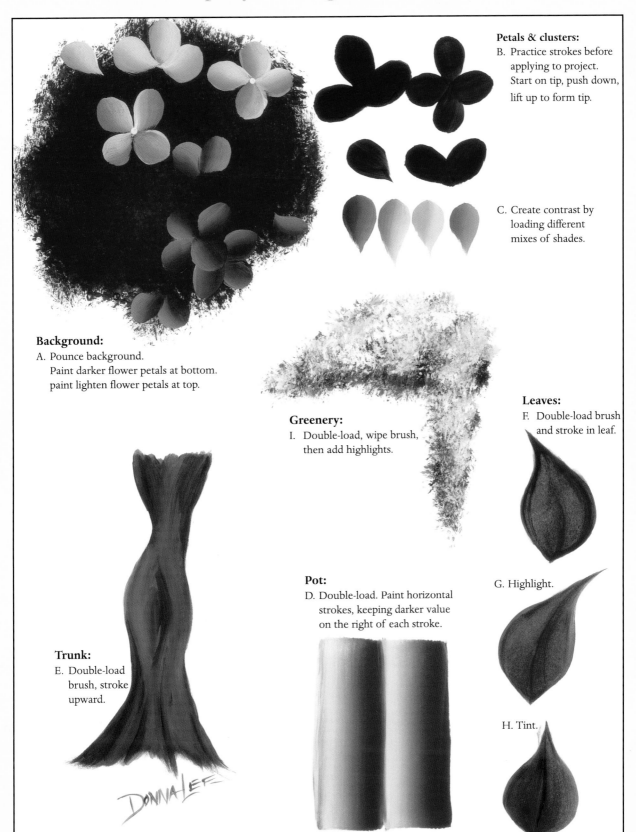

Petals & clusters:
B. Practice strokes before applying to project. Start on tip, push down, lift up to form tip.

C. Create contrast by loading different mixes of shades.

Background:
A. Pounce background. Paint darker flower petals at bottom. paint lighten flower petals at top.

Greenery:
I. Double-load, wipe brush, then add highlights.

Leaves:
F. Double-load brush and stroke in leaf.

G. Highlight.

H. Tint.

Trunk:
E. Double-load brush, stroke upward.

Pot:
D. Double-load. Paint horizontal strokes, keeping darker value on the right of each stroke.

DonnaLee

What you need to get started:

Painting surfaces:
Small galvanized trash can & lid

Enamel paints:
Berry Wine
Dioxazine Purple
Hunter Green
Licorice
School Bus Yellow
Sunflower
Thicket
Wicker White
Yellow Ochre

Brushes:
Flats: #12, ¾"
Script liner: #2
Scruffies: ¼", ½"

Additional supplies:
Aerosol sealer, gloss
Palette
Sea sponge
Vinegar

How do I paint from a painting worksheet?

Sometimes a pattern is not given with a project because the painting worksheets sufficiently show each element and technique. If you do not feel comfortable painting without a pattern, trace the worksheets to make your own pattern.

Here's how:

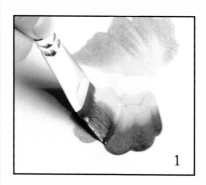

1. Double-load brush with light-value colors. Starting at top of leaf, "wiggle" a base-coat in a circular motion over design, making a scalloped pattern. Bring brush up on the chiseled edge to form point at tip.

2. Repeat for other side of leaf. Repeat on outer edges with medium-value colors.

3. Double-load brush with dark-value colors and repeat wiggle strokes on middle of leaf.

Garden Trash Can

Designed by Terri Ridenour

Using the technique:

1. Refer to *General instructions—prepare* on pages 14–18. Prepare metal areas to be painted.

2. Double-load sponge with Thicket and Wicker White. Sponge background randomly ⅓ of the way up can. Sponge top of lid. Let dry.

3. Refer to *General instructions— paint design* on pages 19–22. Refer to Leaves & Moss Painting Worksheet on page 99. Double-load ¾" flat with Thicket and Sunflower. Paint stems for hollyhock first, then stems for black-eyed Susans. Fill in between with five-petal flower stems and small-leafed greenery stems.

4. With same colors and brush, paint large and medium-sized leaves. Some leaves may be painted with Thicket plus Wicker White. *Note: Small leaves will be added after all flowers are painted.*

5. Refer to Garden Painting Worksheet on pages 100–101. Double-load ¾" flat with Berry Wine and Wicker White. With white to the outside edge, paint hollyhock petals and buds.

6. Double-load ½" scruffy with Wicker White and Yellow Ochre. Pounce flower centers.

7. Using liner, outline flower centers with inky Licorice.

8. Double-load #12 flat with School Bus Yellow and Yellow Ochre. Paint black-eyed Susan petals from outside edge to center.

9. Double-load ½" scruffy with Berry Wine and Yellow Ochre. Pounce flower centers.

10. Double-load #12 flat with Dioxazine Purple and Wicker White. Using chiseled edge and starting at top of wildflower stems, paint flowers working downward.

11. Double-load #12 flat with Berry Wine and Wicker White. With Berry Wine turned upward, pounce dab flowers on chiseled edge of brush.

12. Double-load #12 flat with Dioxazine Purple and Wicker White. With white to outside edge, paint five-petal flowers.

13. Using handle end of brush, dot five-petal flower centers with School Bus Yellow.

14. Refer to Leaves & Moss Painting Worksheet on page 99. Double-load #12 flat with Sunflower and Thicket. Paint single-stroke leaves.

15. Refer to Garden Painting Worksheet on pages 100–101. Double-load with Hunter Green and Wicker White. Paint hummingbird back.

16. Double-load with Berry Wine and Wicker White. Paint front of bird.

17. Double-load with Hunter Green and Wicker White, paint wings and tail.

18. Using liner, paint eye and beak with inky Licorice.

19. Dot highlights on eye and base of beak with Wicker White.

20. Using ½" scruffy pounce bees' bodies with Yellow Ochre. Let dry.

21. Using liner, paint stripes, legs, antennae, and stingers with inky Licorice.

22. Double-load #12 flat with School Bus Yellow and Wicker White. Paint butterfly wings.

23. Load liner with inky Licorice. Paint butterfly body and antennas.

24. Refer to Leaves & Moss Painting Worksheet on page 99. Double-load ¾" scruffy with Sunflower and Thicket. With Thicket on top, pounce moss. Let dry.

25. Refer to *General instructions—finish* on page 23. Sign project.

26. Apply 2–3 coats of aerosol sealer. Let dry between coats.

Leaves & Moss Painting Worksheet

Large leaves:

B. Start at top of leaf, wiggle in circular motion to form outer edge. Come up on chiseled edge to end leaf with a point. Repeat on other side of leaf.

C. Using chiseled edge to form stem and vein. Pull toward center.

E. Using chiseled edge to form stem and vein. Pull toward center.

Single-stroke leaves:

F. Double-load. Pull and lift up on chiseled edge.

Medium leaves:

D. Using smaller brush and less pressure than large leaves, wiggle in and out to form each half leaf.

G. Using chiseled edge, pull stems toward center.

Stem:

A. Using chiseled edge, pull lines upward.

Moss:

H. Double-load. Pounce, keeping lighter value toward bottom.

99

Hollyhock:

A. Wiggle in a circular motion with a double-loaded brush.

Center:

D. Pounce center, then outline with inky paint.

B. Paint overlapping petals, leaving open area for center.

Bud:

C. Start at top and paint in overlapping sections.

I. Stroke stems upward, connecting to petals.

Wildflowers:

J. Double-load. Touch, pull, and lift.

K. Paint overlapping petals.

N. Paint overlapping petals.

O. Dot flower center.

Five-petal flower:

M. Double-load. Touch, pull, and lift.

Dab flowers:

L. Double-load, then pounce once on chiseled edge.

Q. Start at top and paint front of bird.

Butterfly:

U. Double-load. Make circular motion without lifting brush.

V. Stroke body line and antennae with inky paint.

T. Add wings and antennae.

Hummingbird:

P. Double-load. Wiggle back of bird.

S. Stroke in head and tail.

Bee:

R. Pounce body.

G. Stroke toward center.

Black-eyed Susan:

E. Touch, pull, and lift on chiseled-edge to form petal.

H. Pounce center with double-loaded brush.

Moss:

W. Pounce randomly, starting at top of flower.

F. Continue to make petals next to one another.

101

Section 4: The gallery

Vines Table & Wall Border
designed by Kathi Malarchuk

Ivy & Bird
designed by Kathi Malarchuk

Ultra Classic Master Bedroom
designed by Donna Dewberry

Gigi's Garden Patio Table
designed by Gigi Smith-Burns

Birdhouses & Dogwood Potting Bench
designed by Chris Stokes

Zoo Bed Accessories
designed by Alison Stillwell

Potted Herbs Cabinet
designed by Kathi Malarchuk

Metric equivalency chart

inches to millimetres and centimetres (mm-millimetres   cm-centimetres)

inches	mm	cm	inches	cm	inches	cm	inches	cm
⅛	3	0.3	6	15.2	21	53.3	36	91.4
¼	6	0.6	7	17.8	22	55.9	37	94.0
⅜	10	1.0	8	20.3	23	58.4	38	96.5
½	13	1.3	9	22.9	24	61.0	39	99.1
⅝	16	1.6	10	25.4	25	63.5	40	101.6
¾	19	1.9	11	27.9	26	66.0	41	104.1
⅞	22	2.2	12	30.5	27	68.6	42	106.7
1	25	2.5	13	33.0	28	71.1	43	109.2
1¼	32	3.2	14	35.6	29	73.7	44	111.8
1½	38	3.8	15	38.1	30	76.2	45	114.3
1¾	44	4.4	16	40.6	31	78.7	46	116.8
2	51	5.1	17	43.2	32	81.3	47	119.4
3	76	7.6	18	45.7	33	83.8	48	121.9
4	102	10.2	19	48.3	34	86.4	49	124.5
5	127	12.7	20	50.8	35	88.9	50	127.0

Index